Chocolate on the Brain

Chocolate on the Brain

Foolproof Recipes for Unrepentant Chocoholics

Kevin Mills and Nancy Mills

Illustrations by Greg Clarke

Houghton Mifflin Company

Boston ★ New York ★ 2000

For information about permission to reproduce selections
from this book, write to Permissions, Houghton Mifflin Company,
215 Park Avenue South, New York, New York 10003.

Visit our Web site: www.hmco.com/trade.

Library of Congress Cataloging-in-Publication Data
Mills, Kevin.
Chocolate on the brain : foolproof recipes for unrepentant chocoholics /
Kevin Mills and Nancy Mills ; illustrations by Greg Clarke.
p. cm.
ISBN 0-395-98358-4
1. Cookery (Chocolate). 2. Desserts. I. Mills, Nancy, 1942– . II. Title.
TX767.C5.M55 2000
641.6'374 dc21
00-061323

Designed by Lisa Diercks
The text of this book is set in Columbus, Scala Sans, and Dolores.

Printed in the United States of America
QUM 10 9 8 7 6 5 4 3 2 1

To Jody, whom I love even more than chocolate

To Joey, who smeared his first piece of chocolate cake all over his face

And to my college gang: Adam, Hillary, Jennifer, Mike, Patty, Paul, Scott and Tara—I love you all.

    — K.M.

Thanks to Bonnie: To write is human; to edit, divine.

Thanks to Bart: To cook is fun; to eat, hard work.

    — N.M.

Special thanks to: Honey Albino, Maureen Clune, Dominic Crapart, Steve Dunhoff, Barry Estabrook, Lynne Giviskos, Sue Hagen, Margie King, Joan, Dick and Dan Kraft, Deborah Krasner, Laurel Lambert, Annie Lindenfield, Rux Martin, Carol Mead, Martha Mills, Sue Prochnik, Julie Riskin, Judy Rich, Donald Russell, Dorothy Samuel, Tom Trenga and Sharon Rank Ward.

Most of the historical data for the timelines is based on information in *The True History of Chocolate*, by Sophie D. Coe and Michael D. Coe (1996), and *The Emperors of Chocolate*, by Joël Glenn Brenner (1999). They are both well researched and worth reading if your interest in chocolate extends to the fanatical. I also found useful information in: *All About Chocolate*, by Carole Bloom (1998), *Chocolate Fads, Folklore & Fantasies*, by Linda K. Fuller, Ph.D. (1994), *Chocolate from A to Z*, by Katherine Khodorowsky and Hervé Robert (1997), *Chocolate: An Illustrated History*, by Marcia and Frederick Morton (1986), *The World Encyclopedia of Food*, by L. Patrick Coyle (1982) and *The Dictionary of American Food and Drink*, by John F. Mariani (1983).

Contents

Introduction ★ xi

Quick Relief for Chocoholics ★ xv

Chocolate for Breakfast ★ 2

Cakes/Cupcakes/Icings ★ 28

Cookies/Brownies ★ 74

Pies/Pie Crusts ★ 136

Mousses/Puddings/Soufflés ★ 166

Chocolate with Fruit/Ice Cream ★ 188

Sauces ★ 230

Candy ★ 240

Drinks ★ 254

Questions Beginning Chocoholics Often Ask ★ 263

Baking Basics Mom Taught Me ★ 270

Key Weights & Measures ★ 278

Index ★ 280

About the Authors ★ 286

Introduction

I don't trust people who say they don't like chocolate. To me, it's like saying you don't much care for oxygen, or you're tired of living aboveground. I just can't relate to people like that. They should be closely monitored, if not rounded up and reeducated. But I guess they would say the same thing about me.

Why do I and so many other people love chocolate so much? Maybe it's because it makes us feel like kids. At the advancing age of twenty-seven, that's important to me. To eat chocolate is to remember what eating was like before you'd even heard of vitamins, before food had any consequences. If it tasted good, you ate a lot of it; if it didn't, you hid it in your napkin. As an adult you're supposed to eat five servings of vegetables a day. If I ate that many vegetables, my face would break out in broccoli florets. A little chocolate excess keeps me from becoming an adult sourpuss.

There are a lot of ways to get the chocolate fix you need in this day and age. You can stand in the checkout line and endure the sarcastic smile of the clerk as he scans your Snickers bar; you can avoid any of the shame associated with adult chocolate consumption by seeking out isolated vending machines; or you can invest your hard-earned money in an overpriced box of truffles or a paper-thin slice of chocolate cheesecake at a fancy restaurant. I'm likely to do all of those in a single afternoon. But there is another way—a tastier, cheaper, much-bigger-serving way: cooking it yourself.

Making your own chocolate desserts is not like regular cooking. There's none of the responsible, practical maturity that's required to make a meal of asparagus, okra and turkey burgers. No, cooking with chocolate is about eliminating the middleman. It's about licking the bowl and stuffing your face, and—but only if you're feeling saintly—sharing with others.

I took an indirect route to baking. Being lazy, I'd fended off all of my mom's offers to teach me how to cook while I was growing up. But one night when my parents were out, I had a severe chocolate attack. I was almost at the point of eating a bag of brown sugar when I decided to try making chocolate chip cookies. I'd seen Mom make them lots of times, so it felt natural to dump the ingredients into the food processor and then put the batter in the oven. (The closest my dad had ever come to baking was pouring a bag of flour on his brother's head when he was six.)

When my parents returned and saw me eating cookies on the couch, my mom was as proud as if I'd taken my first steps. "Our son's baking!" she said to Dad, shedding a tear. Dad, who'd watched me strike out in all one hundred at-bats I'd had that season in Little League, was glad I could do anything. We sat and ate cookies, and rejoiced.

It took me a decade to bake anything else. I'm not really adventurous, so whenever I'd crave a chocolate dessert I'd think, "How 'bout some chocolate chip cookies?" But I eventually broadened my horizons. My mom, who's a chocolate fanatic in her own right, continually experimented with new concoctions. She'd occasionally hand me a recipe for something like Chocolate Mousse or Almost-Flourless

Chocolate Cake. I'd cook them and sometimes offer her a suggestion or two on how to improve them, such as, "Add more chocolate." Now, a couple years down the road, I've developed quite a repertoire of chocolate desserts. They range from simple treats that I can enjoy before my morning orange juice to weapons-grade feasts that leave me lying on the couch with my belt undone.

In this book, my mom and I share our passion for chocolate with the world. If you share our unbridled obsession, you've come to the right place. But beware: This isn't a book for people who like to nibble, who can eat just one piece of chocolate and move on. This book is for those poor souls enslaved by chocolate, who sit at work and think about chocolate, who hatch plots to get other people's chocolate, who buy their loved ones gifts of chocolate only to consume them themselves—who can stand any torture, sit through any sitcom, but are rendered powerless by chocolate as if it were Kryptonite. If I'm talking to you, you need not be ashamed of your feelings for chocolate. And if you are, just close the blinds.

—KEVIN MILLS

Quick Relief for Chocoholics

Patience is a virtue. I don't happen to have it, and if you don't either, you should choose these recipes, which can be ready to eat in 35 minutes or less. But if you're satisfied by licking the bowl, just about any recipe will do.

10 MINUTES OR LESS
Instant Chocolate Mousse Fix ★ 174
Low-Fat Creamy Chocolate Yogurt ★ 176
Bittersweet Dessert Sauce ★ 232
Chocolate Syrup ★ 236
Hot Fudge Sauce ★ 238

15 MINUTES
Ganache ★ 70
Incredibly Easy Chocolate Mousse (if you let it
    cool only 5 minutes) ★ 172
Chocolate-Mocha Sauce ★ 234
Parisian Hot Chocolate ★ 256
Mexican Hot Chocolate ★ 258
Untraditional Chocolate Soda ★ 260

20–25 MINUTES
Quick Fudge Icing ★ 72
Traditional Chocolate Chip Cookies ★ 93
Chocolate Crispy Rice Treats ★ 132
Chocolate Fondue ★ 192

30–35 MINUTES
Chocolate Chip Muffins ★ 6
Chocolate Chip Scones ★ 8
Chocolate Coconut Macaroons ★ 80
Chocolate Thumbprints ★ 82
Chocolate Chip Peanut Butter Cookies ★ 99
No-Bake Chocolate Granola Bars ★ 134
Real Chocolate Pudding ★ 186
Chocolate Almond Crunch ★ 248
Peanut Butter and Chocolate Chunks ★ 250

Chocolate on the Brain

Chocolate for Breakfast

If you're the type of person who's mad at the world the second the alarm goes off, if your stale coffee reminds you of your boss's bad breath, if the dryness of your toast makes you think of the promotion you didn't get and if the only joy you have to look forward to is cutting off a hearse on your way to work, you need to start your day with chocolate. Forget the lumpy oatmeal and give yourself a Chocolate Waffle or Chocolate Chip Muffin. Your co-workers will thank you.

Chocolate Banana Bread ★ 4

Chocolate Chip Muffins ★ 6

Chocolate Chip Scones ★ 8

Chocolate Chip Mini-Bagels ★ 10

Chocolate-Filled Baby Brioches ★ 14

Orange-Chocolate Breakfast Cake ★ 18

Chocolate Waffles ★ 22

Chocolate Chip Rugelach ★ 25

Chocolate Banana Bread

Serves: 12–16 ⏱ Preparation time: 10–15 minutes 🕯 Baking time: 60–70 minutes ⚖ Rating: Easy

Once when I was young, I tried to get my grandmother to buy Chocolate Chip Cookie Cereal. When she asked if my mother would approve, I said, "Of course," pointing out that it had two essential vitamins and one pretty important mineral. I finished the whole box before my mom came back. Now that I'm older and I can buy whatever cereal I want, I usually choose to skip breakfast. But Chocolate Banana Bread is a great way to lure me to the table. Besides, bananas are good for you, right?

6 tablespoons unsalted butter, softened to room temperature, + more for greasing
1¾ cups all-purpose flour + 1 teaspoon for dusting pan
1 cup sugar
2 ripe bananas

🐭 Mom Tip
Regular chocolate
chips can also be
used.

2 large eggs
1 teaspoon vanilla extract
¼ cup milk
½ cup unsweetened cocoa powder
2 teaspoons baking powder
½ teaspoon salt
1 cup chopped walnuts
1 cup semisweet mini chocolate chips (see Mom Tip)

Place an oven rack in the middle position and preheat the oven to 350°. Lightly rub the bottom and sides of a 9-x-5-inch bread pan with butter. Add the 1 teaspoon flour and swirl it around, coating the buttered surfaces. To make it easier to remove the bread, cut a piece of wax paper to fit the bottom of the pan. Place it in the pan and wipe it with butter. Set aside.

Put the butter and sugar in a large bowl, and beat with an electric mixer or a wooden spoon until creamy. Mash the bananas, add to the bowl and mix until well combined. Add the eggs, vanilla and milk, and mix again. Add the flour, cocoa, baking powder and salt and mix until well blended. Add the nuts and chocolate chips and mix thoroughly. The mixture will be thick and lumpy.

Pour the batter into the pan, and spread evenly. Bake for 60 to 70 minutes, or until the bread pulls away from the sides and a cake tester or knife inserted into the center comes out clean. Remove from the oven, and cool for 10 minutes. Loosen the bread by sliding a knife around the sides of the pan. Transfer the loaf to a cooling rack, and cool to room temperature. Slice thinly and serve. Store in the refrigerator, wrapped in foil or plastic wrap.

Chocolate Chip Muffins

Makes: 10 muffins ⏱ Preparation time: 20 minutes 🕯 Baking time: 15 minutes ✎ Rating: Very Easy

---

Mom Tip 1
To make richer muffins, substitute heavy cream or sour cream for the milk.

Mom Tip 2
Combining two different kinds of chocolate chips is nice but not necessary for these muffins. Instead, use 1 cup of whichever type of chocolate chip you prefer.

$\mathcal{S}$ome people get excited by blueberry muffins. Others have to eat bran muffins on doctor's orders. Not me. If I'm going to eat something as healthy as a muffin, there'd better be some chocolate in it.

¼ cup (½ stick) unsalted butter
⅓ cup milk (see Mom Tip 1)
1 large egg
½ teaspoon vanilla extract
1 cup all-purpose flour
3 tablespoons sugar
3 tablespoons brown sugar
1 teaspoon baking powder
¼ teaspoon salt

½ cup semisweet chocolate chips
½ cup milk chocolate chips (see Mom Tip 2)

Melt the butter in a small pot over low heat. Set aside to cool.

Place an oven rack in the middle position and preheat the oven to 400°. Place 10 paper cupcake liners in a 12-cup muffin pan (see Mom Tip 3). Set aside.

Put the butter, milk, egg and vanilla in a medium bowl, and beat with a fork for about 30 seconds, or until the mixture is well combined.

Combine the flour, the sugars, baking powder and salt in a large bowl, and mix with a large spoon (see Mom Warning). Add the milk mixture and stir until just combined. The muffin batter should be slightly lumpy. Stir in both kinds of chocolate chips.

Spoon the mixture evenly into each cupcake liner, filling them about two-thirds full. Bake for about 15 minutes, or until the muffins are firm to the touch and are beginning to brown. Remove from the oven, and cool in the pan for a few minutes, then lift them out by hand onto a cooling rack. If they stick, slide a knife around the outer edges to loosen them from the pan. Serve warm or at room temperature.

Chocolate Chip Scones

Makes: 8 scones ⏲ Preparation time: 15 minutes 🔥 Baking time: 15–20 minutes 🥄 Rating: Very Easy

~~~~~~

*E*nglish cooking has an unfortunate reputation. For decades, tourists have been grousing about steak and kidney pie, custard and toad-in-the-hole for being food that will keep you alive but won't give you a reason to live. Perhaps that's why the English have such an incredible sweet tooth — anything to get the taste of bad dinners out of their mouths. But scones are one English food I'm very fond of. And Chocolate Chip Scones are good enough for both the queen and the chocoholic.

¼	cup (½ stick) unsalted butter, softened to room temperature, + more for greasing
1¾	cups all-purpose flour
1	tablespoon sugar + ½ teaspoon for topping
2¼	teaspoons baking powder
½	teaspoon salt
2	large eggs

⨉ Mom Tip
To make individual
scones, separate the
wedges so that they
are at least ½ inch
apart and bake for 12
to 15 minutes.

⅓   cup heavy cream
½   cup chocolate chips

Place an oven rack in the middle position and preheat the oven to 425°. Lightly rub a cookie sheet with butter. Set aside.

Put the butter in a large bowl, and beat with an electric mixer or a wooden spoon until smooth and creamy. Add the flour, sugar, baking powder and salt and mix or beat on low speed just until blended. Add the eggs and cream, and mix just until the dough begins to come together in a ball. Stir in the chocolate chips. The mixture will be very thick and lumpy. Do not mix the batter too much, or the scones will be tough.

Transfer the dough to the cookie sheet, and pat into a 7- or 8-inch circle about ¾ inch thick. Cut the circle into 8 equal sections, but don't separate them (see Mom Tip). Sprinkle ½ teaspoon sugar over the top and bake for 15 to 20 minutes, or until the top is golden brown. It will look like a giant biscuit. Remove from the oven, and cool on the cookie sheet for 10 minutes. Then transfer the scone to a rack, and cool to room temperature. Break the scone into the 8 wedges, following the knife marks. Serve on a large plate with or without butter and jam.

Chocolate Chip Mini-Bagels

Makes: 16 mini-bagels ⏱ Preparation time: 15–25 minutes (15 if you use a food processor) ✋ Rising time: 1 hour 🔥 Baking time: 15–20 minutes ⚖ Rating: Not So Easy

~~~~~~

Chocolate Chip Mini-Bagels are like breakfast chocolate chip cookies. Because they're not overly sweet, they're a good way to ease into your chocolate day.

My mom likes to eat them right out of the oven, while the chocolate's still gooey. Unfortunately, the bagels are 400 degrees at that point. So she holds one in her asbestos gloves, waiting for the first second she can bite into it without igniting her lips.

        ¼ cup (½ stick) unsalted butter + more for greasing
      1¼ cups water
        2 tablespoons sugar
        1 ¼-ounce package active dry yeast
        1 large egg

☼! Mom Warning 1
Yeast is a living organism, and high temperatures will kill it. Before combining any heated liquid with yeast, test a drop on the back of your hand to make sure it is no hotter than lukewarm.

4–5 cups all-purpose flour
1 teaspoon salt
1 teaspoon corn or vegetable oil
1 cup (6-ounce package) semisweet chocolate chips

Melt the butter in a small pot over low heat. Set aside to cool.

Heat the water briefly in a kettle or pot, just to take the chill off. It should be no more than lukewarm (see Mom Warning 1).

USING A FOOD PROCESSOR OR AN ELECTRIC MIXER WITH A DOUGH HOOK: Pour the water into the appliance bowl. Sprinkle the sugar and yeast into the water, and stir for a few seconds until the yeast dissolves. Let the mixture sit for about 5 minutes, or until it becomes frothy. Beat the egg, and add to the mixture. Add the butter, and mix to incorporate. Add 3½ cups of the flour and the salt, and process, or beat on slow speed, adding more flour as necessary, ½ cup at a time, until the dough stops being sticky and becomes smooth and satiny. In a food processor, this takes about 1 minute; in a mixer, 5 to 6 minutes.

MIXING BY HAND: Pour the water into a large bowl. Sprinkle the sugar and yeast into the water, and stir for a few seconds until the yeast dissolves. Let the mixture sit for about 5 minutes, or until it becomes frothy. Beat the egg and add to the mixture. Add the butter and mix to incorporate. Add 3½ cups of the flour and the salt, and mix with a wooden spoon. Sprinkle ½ cup flour onto a dry, clean work surface and carefully transfer the dough onto the flour. Knead the dough by folding it over and over on itself while pushing it with your hands for 8 to 10 minutes, gradually adding more flour as necessary, ½ cup at a time, until the dough is smooth and satiny.

☞ Mom Tip
Use kitchen scissors
to cut the dough.

Pour 1 teaspoon oil into a large bowl, and spread around with a paper towel, making sure to grease the sides as well as the bottom. Place the kneaded dough in the bowl and turn over so that the top is greased. Cover the bowl with a clean towel or put it inside a plastic bag, and set aside on the counter for the dough to rise for 1 hour. When it has risen, fill a large pot at least half full of hot tap water, cover and begin heating over high heat.

Place one oven rack in the top position and the other in the bottom position and preheat the oven to 400°. Lightly rub two cookie sheets with butter. Set aside.

Take the risen dough out of the bowl, knead a few times to get the air pockets out and divide into 16 equal pieces (see Mom Tip).

Spread a clean tea towel on the counter. Take 1 piece of dough and 1 tablespoon of the chocolate chips (about 15) and knead them together. Then roll the dough between your hands into a cylinder about 6 inches long and ½ inch thick. Overlap the ends and pinch together tightly to make a ring. Or simply make a 1-inch hole in the center of the dough, and shape into a ring. Make sure the chocolate chips are not exposed. Lay the ring on the tea towel. Repeat the process until you have 16 rings.

When the pot of water has come to a boil, gently pick up a dough ring, and drop into the water. Drop 3 more in, one by one, and let cook for about 1 minute. They will puff up and double in size. Gently turn them over with a metal spatula and let cook for another minute. Transfer the bagels with a slotted spoon to one cookie sheet and boil another 4. Transfer those to the same cookie sheet and bake on the top rack for 15 to 20 minutes, or until the tops are golden brown.

While the first batch is baking, boil the second batch, as before. Transfer them to the second cookie sheet and begin baking them on the bottom rack of the oven. When you remove the first cookie sheet from the oven, transfer the second cookie sheet from the bottom rack to the top rack to finish baking. The bagels brown better on the top rack.

When the bagels are done, remove from the oven and transfer to a rack to cool. Serve warm or at room temperature, or reheat for 5 minutes in a 350° oven (see Mom Warning 2). Store in the refrigerator in an airtight container or wrapped in foil or plastic wrap.

1375–1521 Since the Aztecs value cacao beans highly as a beverage and as currency, counterfeit beans become a real menace. The phony beans are generally made of clay and are used in trade throughout the empire. Counterfeit beans are still a problem today, as anyone who's tasted carob can attest.

Chocolate-Filled Baby Brioches

Makes: 12 brioches 🕐 Preparation time: 30–40 minutes ✋ Rising time: 2½ hours or overnight
🔥 Baking time: 12–15 minutes 🥄 Rating: Not So Easy

In the United States, you actually have to get in your car and drive to the chocolate, but in Paris there's a chocolatier on virtually every street. Chocolate-filled brioches were my favorite discovery there. It's the high-brow French version of the jelly doughnut, with chocolate in the middle. This is our mini-version.

    ¼ cup milk
    2 tablespoons sugar
    1 ¼-ounce package active dry yeast
  2¼ cups all-purpose flour + more if needed
    ½ teaspoon salt

🖙 Mom Tip 1
If the dough won't
stick together, add 1
or 2 tablespoons
water. If the dough is
so sticky it clings to
your hands, add 1 or 2
tablespoons flour, or
even more if
necessary.

½ cup (1 stick) unsalted butter, softened to room temperature,
+ more for greasing

2 large eggs

6 squares (6 ounces) semisweet chocolate

GLAZE

2 tablespoons milk

2 tablespoons sugar

Heat the milk briefly in a small pot, just to take the chill off. It should be no more than lukewarm.

USING A FOOD PROCESSOR OR AN ELECTRIC MIXER WITH A DOUGH HOOK: Pour the milk into the appliance bowl. Sprinkle the sugar and yeast into the milk, and stir for a few seconds until the yeast dissolves. Let the mixture sit for about 5 minutes, or until it becomes frothy. Add the flour and salt, and process or beat on low speed. Add the butter and eggs, and continue processing or beating until the dough rolls itself into a ball (see Mom Tip 1). The dough will be slightly sticky. In a food processor, this takes about 1 minute; in a mixer, 5 to 6 minutes.

MIXING BY HAND: Combine the sugar, yeast and milk in a large bowl and stir for a few seconds until the yeast dissolves. Let the mixture sit for about 5 minutes, or until it becomes frothy. Beat in the butter and eggs. Add the flour and salt, and stir well with a wooden spoon until the dough can be formed into a rough ball. The dough will be slightly sticky (see Mom Tip 1). Sprinkle 1 tablespoon flour onto a cutting board or another clean, flat surface. Place the dough on the floured

Mom Tip 2
To ensure that your
yeast dough rises
successfully, keep it
covered to ward off
drafts, and leave it on
the counter or put in
an unheated oven
with the heat off.

surface and knead it by folding it over and over on itself while pushing it with your hands for 8 to 10 minutes, or until the dough is smooth and satiny. Add 1 or 2 more tablespoons flour if the dough sticks to your hands. Shape it into a ball.

Using a paper towel, rub the inside of a large bowl with ½ teaspoon butter, making sure to grease the sides as well as the bottom. Put the dough into the bowl, cover with a clean dish towel or plastic wrap, and set aside on the kitchen counter for 2 hours, or until it has doubled in size (see Mom Tip 2). Or you can refrigerate it overnight, wrapped in plastic.

Cut each chocolate square in half. Set aside. Lightly rub a 12-cup muffin pan or a cookie sheet with butter.

If you have refrigerated the dough overnight, let it sit out at room temperature for 30 minutes before proceeding. Punch down the dough with your fist to get rid of any air pockets. Divide it into 12 equal pieces. Flatten each piece into a circle slightly bigger than the chocolate. Place a piece of chocolate in the center of each circle and tightly pinch the edges of the dough together to enclose the chocolate. Shape each piece of dough into a ball with your fingers and place, pinched edges down, in the muffin pan or on the cookie sheet. Cover with a clean dish towel or plastic wrap and set aside on the kitchen counter for about 30 minutes, or until the balls have doubled in size.

Meanwhile, place an oven rack in the middle position and preheat the oven to 400°.

TO MAKE THE GLAZE: Combine the milk and sugar in a small pot, and bring to a boil, stirring with a wooden spoon, over high heat. Remove from the heat and gently spoon a little of the glaze over each brioche.

Bake the brioches for 12 to 15 minutes, or until they have puffed and the tops are light brown and shiny. Serve warm. Reheat, if necessary, in a 325° oven for 10 minutes, so the chocolate will be warm and gooey.

Orange-Chocolate Breakfast Cake

Serves: 10–12 Preparation time: 20 minutes + 2½ hours, if using homemade Candied Orange Peel
Baking time: 45–50 minutes Rating: Easy

My mom and I went on a chocolate research trip to London last year. We ate chocolate for breakfast, lunch and dinner. There are worse ways to spend a vacation. We came across this breakfast cake at Selfridges, an upscale department store. The cake looks like a fancy loaf of bread but tastes a little like orange gingerbread. It was our favorite discovery on the trip, and we figured out how to make it when we got home.

Mom Tip 1
You can usually find candied orange peel in small bags near the dried fruit in supermarkets or in candy stores. It is easy but time-consuming to make (see page 21).

CAKE

¾ cup (1½ sticks) unsalted butter, softened to room temperature, + more for greasing

1 cup all-purpose flour + 1 teaspoon for dusting pan

⅔ cup candied orange peel (see Mom Tip 1)

1 cup sugar

3 large eggs

1 teaspoon vanilla extract

¼ cup unsweetened cocoa powder

1 teaspoon baking powder

½ teaspoon salt

ORANGE GLAZE

½ cup powdered sugar

1 tablespoon orange juice + more if needed

Place an oven rack in the middle position and preheat the oven to 350°. Lightly rub the bottom and sides of a 9-x-5-inch bread pan with butter. Add the 1 teaspoon flour and swirl it around, coating the buttered surfaces. To make it easier to remove the cake from the pan, cut a piece of wax paper to fit the bottom of the pan. Place it in the pan, and wipe it with butter. Set aside.

Chop the orange peel into ¼-inch pieces. Set aside.

TO MAKE THE CAKE: Put the butter and sugar in a large bowl, and beat with an electric mixer or a wooden spoon until smooth and creamy. Add the eggs and vanilla, and beat on low speed until well incorporated. Add the flour, cocoa, baking powder and salt, and beat on low speed just until blended. Do not beat the batter too much, or the cake will be tough. By hand, stir in the chopped pieces of candied orange peel and mix thoroughly.

Pour the batter into the pan and bake for 45 to 50 minutes, or until the top is firm and a toothpick or cake tester inserted into the center comes out clean.

MEANWHILE, MAKE THE GLAZE: Combine the powdered sugar and orange juice in a small pan. Stir until the sugar dissolves. Heat for about 1 minute over low heat, or until the mixture begins bubbling around the edges. If the glaze won't pour easily, add another teaspoon orange juice.

When the cake has finished baking, remove it from the oven and cool on a rack for about 10 minutes. Loosen the cake by sliding a knife around the edges. Place the rack on top of the cake and, with a pot holder in each hand, turn the cake pan and rack over together. If the cake won't come out, turn the pan back over and insert a plastic or rubber spatula between the outer edge of the cake and the pan and gently rock it back and forth until the cake loosens. Remove the wax paper from the bottom of the cake.

Turn the cake right side up and pour the glaze over the cake (see Mom Tip 2). Cool to room temperature. Just before serving, transfer the cake to a plate and slice thinly.

Candied Orange Peel

Makes: 1½ cups ⏲ Preparation time: 30 minutes 🔥 Cooking time: 2 hours ⚖ Rating: Easy

~~~~~~

  2 oranges
  ¾ cup sugar
  ½ cup water

Remove the peels from the oranges in four large sections. With a spoon, scrape away and discard the bitter white pith attached to the orange peel. Cut the peel into long, ¼-inch-wide strips.

Put the strips in a heavy, medium pot, cover with water and bring to a boil over high heat. Reduce the heat to medium and cook, uncovered, for 1 hour. Drain the peel and discard the water. Set aside.

Combine the sugar and ½ cup water in the medium pot and bring to a boil over high heat. Stir constantly, until the sugar dissolves and the liquid is clear. Turn down the heat to low, add the peel and cook, uncovered, for 1 hour, stirring occasionally. The liquid will be almost gone by the end. Watch it carefully during the final 15 minutes so that it doesn't burn. If all the liquid evaporates before the hour is up, immediately remove the orange peel from the heat.

Drain the peel in a strainer, stirring it with a fork to keep the strands from clumping together. Transfer to a large plate, and let cool for 10 minutes, or until it reaches room temperature. The candied peel will be pale orange and covered with sugar. Store at room temperature in a closed container or wrapped in foil or plastic. It will keep for several weeks.

Chocolate Waffles

Serves: 6–8 ⏱ Preparation time: 10 minutes + 10 minutes for Raspberry Sauce or 5 minutes for Chocolate Syrup 🔥 Cooking time: 20–25 minutes ⚓ Special equipment: Waffle iron ♨ Rating: Easy

If you don't have a waffle iron, here's a good reason to buy one. With chocolate sauce instead of maple syrup, waffles can become a dessert as well as an overly elaborate brunch that you serve your in-laws.

- 1¾ cups all-purpose flour
- ½ cup sugar
- ½ cup unsweetened cocoa powder
- 2 teaspoons baking powder
- ½ teaspoon salt
- 2 cups buttermilk
- 3 large eggs
- 1 tablespoon corn oil or vegetable oil

Mom Tip
If you are serving Chocolate Waffles for dessert instead of breakfast, ice cream is a good accompaniment.

1   teaspoon vanilla extract
    Raspberry Sauce (page 24) or Chocolate Syrup (page 236)
    Fresh raspberries, strawberries or blueberries
    Rocky Road or vanilla ice cream (optional; see Mom Tip)

Read the directions on your waffle iron. If you need to apply oil or butter before pouring on the batter, do so. If it should be preheated, turn it on.

Combine the flour, sugar, cocoa, baking powder and salt in a large bowl. Add the buttermilk, eggs, oil and vanilla and mix by hand with a large wooden spoon or a whisk, or use an electric mixer. The batter can have a few lumps.

When the waffle iron is hot, pour on the indicated amount of batter. Close the lid and, if there is a lid lock, snap it shut. Under no circumstances should you open the waffle iron during the first minute of cooking, because the waffle will separate. Some waffle irons have a light on the front that stays on until the waffle is done. If your waffle iron is like this, check the waffle only after the light goes out. If there is no light, wait until the steam has stopped coming out of the sides of the waffle iron.

Check the cooked waffle. If it is softer than you like, let it cook for 30 to 60 seconds more to crisp. Serve the waffles immediately, with your sauce of choice, along with some fresh berries. Or keep the cooked waffles warm in a 300° oven while you make the rest of them. Lay them directly on an oven rack, in a single layer, to keep them crisp. Freeze leftovers, wrapped in plastic wrap, and reheat in a toaster.

Raspberry Sauce

Makes: About 1½ cups ⏲ Preparation time: 10 minutes ⟍ Special equipment: Food processor or blender ♨ Rating: Very Easy

~~~~~~

> 1 package (10–12 ounces) thawed frozen raspberries or
> 2 cups fresh raspberries
> 1–2 tablespoons maple syrup or sugar

If using fresh raspberries, rinse them and pat them dry with paper towels.

Put the raspberries and any juice in the bowl of a food processor or blender and process until smooth.

Add 1 tablespoon maple syrup or sugar to the raspberries, and stir. Taste to see if the sauce is sweet enough. If not, add more syrup or sugar until you reach the sweetness you like. Refrigerate, covered, until needed. Serve in a small bowl.

Chocolate Chip Rugelach

Makes: 32 rugelach 🕐 Preparation time: 50 minutes 🕯 Baking time: 40–50 minutes (20–25 minutes per batch) ⚓ Rating: Not So Easy

Rugelach is a traditional Eastern European pastry. The word "traditional" is often a code word for "It tastes bad but we eat it anyway." In that sense, rugelach traditionally consists of nuts and raisins. But when you add chocolate, you'll want more than your share.

🕊 Mom Tip 1
Neufchâtel is a type of
cream cheese that has
one-third less fat than
regular cream cheese.
For a slightly richer
dough, substitute reg-
ular cream cheese.

🕊 Mom Tip 2
Currants are like small
raisins. If you can't
find them at the gro-
cery store, use regular
raisins, but cut them
in half. Full-size
raisins are too big for
these rugelach.

PASTRY

½ cup (1 stick) unsalted butter, softened to room temperature

1 8-ounce package Neufchâtel or light cream cheese,
softened to room temperature (see Mom Tip 1)

¼ cup powdered sugar

2 cups all-purpose flour

¼ teaspoon salt

½ teaspoon vanilla extract

FILLING

⅔ cup chopped walnuts

⅓ cup sugar

½ cup semisweet mini chocolate chips

⅓ cup dried currants (optional; see Mom Tip 2)

1 tablespoon ground cinnamon

To make the pastry: Put the butter, Neufchâtel and powdered sugar in a food processor or a large bowl. Process or beat with an electric mixer until smooth and creamy. Add the flour, salt and vanilla, and process or beat on low speed for about 5 seconds, until the dough rolls itself into a ball, or just until the dough comes together. The dough will be slightly sticky.

Put the dough in a self-sealing plastic bag and refrigerate until you've made the filling. Place an oven rack in the middle position and preheat the oven to 350°.

To make the filling: Combine the walnuts, sugar, mini chocolate chips, currants (if using) and cinnamon in a medium bowl. Set aside.

Set out two cookie sheets but do not grease them.

Remove the dough from the refrigerator, and divide into quarters. Return three of the quarters to the refrigerator. Lay the other quarter on a large sheet of wax paper and flatten it slightly with the heel of your hand. Cover the dough with another large sheet of wax paper and, with a rolling pin, roll it out to a 9-inch circle. Remove the top sheet of wax paper and cut the round into 8 equal wedges.

Sprinkle one-quarter of the filling evenly over the 8 wedges. Then, starting at the outside edge of 1 wedge, roll it carefully toward the center, ending with the point of the wedge wrapped around the pastry. Lay the pastry, point side down, on the ungreased cookie sheet. Repeat with the other 7 wedges. Some of the filling may fall out. If it does, stuff it back in as best you can.

Repeat the process with a second quarter of the dough, making another 8 rugelach. Bake this first batch of 16 rugelach for 20 to 25 minutes, or until they are golden brown. It's better to slightly overbake than to underbake (underbaked rugelach are doughy in the middle). Remove from the oven, and cool on the cookie sheet for about 3 minutes. Then transfer them to a cooling rack.

While the first 16 rugelach are baking, repeat the process above with the other two quarters of dough, making another 16 rugelach.

Serve warm or at room temperature. Store in an airtight container or wrapped in foil or plastic wrap.

Cakes/Cupcakes/ Icings

C akes are all about celebrating. If there's a special event, nobody says, "I'll bring the corn muffins!" Cake is the perfect food to help you forget that you've just turned a year older.

There are more types of chocolate cake than there are bones in the body. Remember Marie Antoinette's famous phrase, "Let them eat cake"? Instead of being outraged, starting a revolution and cutting off her head, the French masses should have simply asked her to be more specific. Did she mean layer cake? Cheesecake? Cupcakes?

Without icing, most cakes can be dry, sad-looking disks of spongy chocolate. But with chocolate goo slathered all over it, a cake will look fresh from the bakery. True beauty may be on the inside, but it doesn't hurt to doll it up a bit.

Overly Indulgent Chocolate Cupcakes ★ 30

Grandma's Chocolate Chip Cupcakes ★ 32

Almost Flourless Chocolate Cake ★ 35

Chocolate Mousse Cake ★ 38

Chocolate Polenta Cake ★ 41

Flourless Chocolate Mocha Cake ★ 44

Chocolate Pound Cake ★ 46

Four-Layer Buttermilk Chocolate Cake ★ 49

You-Deserve-It Fudge Cake ★ 52

Devil's Food Cake ★ 55

Sachertorte ★ 58

Marble Cheesecake ★ 62

Couldn't-Be-Simpler Chocolate Icing ★ 65

Easy Chocolate Glaze ★ 66

Chocolate Buttercream Icing ★ 68

Ganache ★ 70

Quick Fudge Icing ★ 72

1519 After drinking the Aztec chocolate drink at the court of Montezuma, one of Cortés's men announces that chocolate is better suited for pigs than humans. But Cortés himself admires the drink's sustaining power, believing that a man could go all day on just one serving: chocolate as proto-protein shake.

Overly Indulgent Chocolate Cupcakes

Makes: 12 cupcakes ⏰ Preparation time: 15 minutes 🕯 Baking time: 20–25 minutes 🍴 Rating: Easy

~~~~~~

B aking cupcakes makes me feel like June Cleaver on *Leave It to Beaver*. For a twenty-eight-year-old man, that's somewhat distressing. But I get over it once I start indulging myself.

    10 squares (10 ounces) semisweet chocolate
    1¼ cups (2½ sticks) unsalted butter
    ⅓ cup sugar
     5 large eggs
    ⅓ cup all-purpose flour
    ½ teaspoon baking powder
    ¼ teaspoon salt
     1 teaspoon unsweetened cocoa powder

Mom Tip
To keep the cocoa
from clumping, put it
in a small sieve before
dusting the cupcakes
with it. Hold the sieve
over each cupcake
and drag a spoon
through the cocoa, so
that it falls evenly over
each one.

Melt the chocolate and butter in a heavy frying pan over very low heat, stirring constantly. When the chocolate is almost melted, turn off the heat and set aside to cool. The heat of the pan will melt the remaining chocolate.

Place an oven rack in the middle position and preheat the oven to 325°.

Place paper cupcake liners in a 12-cup muffin pan and set aside.

Put the sugar and eggs in a food processor or a large bowl. Process, or beat with an electric mixer for about 2 minutes on high speed until pale yellow and frothy. Add the melted chocolate mixture, and process or beat on low speed until well blended. Add the flour, baking powder and salt, and pulse or beat on low speed just until blended. Do not beat the batter too much, or the cake will be tough.

Spoon the mixture evenly into each cupcake liner. The mixture will fill about two-thirds of each liner. Bake for 20 to 25 minutes, or until the cupcakes are firm to the touch.

Remove the cupcakes from the oven and cool in the pan for a few minutes. Transfer the cupcakes to a cooling rack. Serve warm or at room temperature. Put each cupcake on a small dish and dust with cocoa (see Mom Tip). Store in an airtight container at room temperature.

Grandma's Chocolate Chip Cupcakes

Makes: 12 cupcakes   Preparation time: 30 minutes   Cooking time: 15 minutes   Rating: Easy

My grandma makes these chocolate chip cupcakes every Christmas. We all enjoy them after dinner and then drift to different parts of the house to try to get "Jingle Bells" out of our heads. Then, one by one, we sneak back to the kitchen and try to steal another cupcake from the tin. The tin makes a distinctive rattle, so everyone knows what's going on. Nobody lets on, however, because each of us knows that he or she will be out there next.

CUPCAKES

   ½ cup (1 stick) unsalted butter, softened to room temperature
   ⅓ cup sugar
   ⅓ cup brown sugar
   1 large egg
   ½ teaspoon vanilla extract
   1 cup all-purpose flour

½ teaspoon baking soda
¼ teaspoon salt

TOPPING

½ cup brown sugar
1 large egg
½ teaspoon vanilla extract
 Dash salt
1 cup (6-ounce package) semisweet chocolate chips
½ cup chopped walnuts (optional)

Place an oven rack in the middle position and preheat the oven to 375°. Place paper cupcake liners in a 12-cup muffin pan and set aside (see Mom Tip 3, page 7).

TO MAKE THE CUPCAKES: Put the butter and sugars in a food processor or a large bowl. Process, or beat with an electric mixer until smooth and creamy. Add the egg and vanilla, and process, or beat on low speed until well blended. Add the flour, baking soda and salt, and pulse or beat on low speed just until blended. Do not beat the batter too much, or the cake will be tough.

Divide the batter evenly among the cupcake liners. The batter will fill about half of each liner. Bake for 5 minutes, or until the cupcakes are just beginning to set.

MEANWHILE, MAKE THE TOPPING: Put the brown sugar, egg, vanilla and salt in a medium bowl and mix with a large spoon until combined. Stir in the chocolate chips and, if using, the walnuts.

Remove the partially baked cupcakes from the oven and spoon 1 heaping tablespoon of the filling over each cupcake. Return the cupcakes to the oven and bake for another 10 minutes, or until the tops are firm and beginning to brown.

Remove from the oven and cool in the pan for about 15 minutes. The tops will sink somewhat, so don't be alarmed. Serve warm or at room temperature. Store in an airtight container at room temperature.

Almost Flourless Chocolate Cake

Serves: 8–10 🕙 Preparation time: 20 minutes 🔥 Baking time: 70–80 minutes ✋ Chilling time: 4 hours 🍰 Rating: Easy

~~~~~~

Almost flourless" sounds like "nearly pregnant." But by keeping the flour to a minimum, this cake provides a dense chocolate rush. And just because it's dense doesn't mean you have to eat a smaller piece.

The recipe calls for a "water bath," and when I cooked this cake for the first time, I had to call my mom and ask her what one was. She explained that you need to put the cake pan in a larger pan filled with water so that it cooks more evenly.

Mom Tip
The hot water sur-
rounding the bread
pan helps the batter
cook evenly. Without
it, this cake may be
dry on the outside
and not fully cooked
on the inside.

8 squares (8 ounces) bittersweet or semisweet chocolate
1 cup (2 sticks) unsalted butter + more for greasing
1 teaspoon all-purpose flour + 1 teaspoon for dusting pan
½ cup sugar
4 large eggs
1 pint fresh raspberries (optional)

Melt the chocolate and butter in a heavy frying pan over very low heat, stirring occasionally. When the chocolate is almost melted, turn off the heat and set aside to cool. The heat of the pan will cause the remaining chocolate to melt.

Place an oven rack in the middle position and preheat the oven to 300°. Fill a 9-x-13-inch roasting pan half full of water and place it on the oven rack. Lightly rub the bottom and sides of a 9-x-5-inch bread pan with butter. Add the 1 teaspoon flour and swirl it around to coat the buttered surfaces. To make it easier to remove the cake from the pan, cut a piece of wax paper to fit the bottom of the pan. Place it in the pan and set aside.

Put the sugar, eggs and flour in a food processor or a large bowl. Process, or beat with an electric mixer for about 2 minutes on high speed until pale yellow and frothy. Add the chocolate mixture, and process or beat on low speed until well blended, about 15 seconds.

Pour the batter into the bread pan, and gently place in the middle of the roasting pan; the water will come halfway up the sides of the bread pan (see Mom Tip). Bake for 70 to 80 minutes, or until the top forms a light crust and begins to show tiny cracks and a toothpick or cake tester inserted into the center comes out clean. Remove the bread pan from the water bath and cool on a rack for 30 minutes, or until the cake reaches room temperature. Cover the pan with foil or plastic wrap and refrigerate for at least 4 hours.

If you are using raspberries, rinse them in cold water, drain them thoroughly, pat them dry with paper towels and set aside.

Loosen the cake by sliding a knife around the edges of the pan. If you did not line the pan with wax paper, the cake may not come out of the pan easily. If it sticks, cut it into 8 or 10 slices and with a metal spatula lift each one out gently. Serve individually or on a large platter. Decorate with the raspberries, if using. Store leftovers, covered, in the refrigerator.

Chocolate Mousse Cake

Serves: 8–10 🕙 Preparation time: 30 minutes 🌑 Baking time: 25–30 minutes 🖐 Cooling time: 30 minutes 👍 Rating: Easy

This cake is great for a lazy chocoholic like me. (I'm not lazy when I eat anything chocolate, but I am when I make it.) You don't have to bother with icing, and the recipe is very forgiving. I once substituted powdered sugar for regular sugar, and the cake didn't seem to mind.

    5 squares (5 ounces) bittersweet or semisweet chocolate
    ½ cup (1 stick) unsalted butter, softened to room temperature,
        + more for greasing
    4 large eggs
    ⅓ cup sugar + ¼ cup sugar
    2 tablespoons cornstarch
    1 teaspoon vanilla extract
    ¼ teaspoon salt

½ teaspoon powdered sugar
Raspberry Sauce (page 24; optional)

Melt the chocolate in a small, heavy pot over very low heat, stirring constantly. When the chocolate is almost melted, turn off the heat and set aside to cool. The heat of the pot will melt the remaining chocolate.

Place an oven rack in the middle position and preheat the oven to 325° for a metal or ceramic pie pan or 300° for a glass pie pan. Lightly rub the bottom and sides of a 9-inch pie pan with butter. Set aside.

Separate the eggs, putting the yolks in a small cup and the whites in a large metal or ceramic bowl with no traces of grease. Set aside.

Put the butter and ⅓ cup sugar in a food processor or a large bowl. Process or beat with an electric mixer until smooth and creamy. Add the egg yolks, cornstarch, vanilla and salt, and process, or beat on low speed until well blended. Add the melted chocolate, and process or beat just until blended.

Beat the egg whites with the mixer just until they form stiff peaks. Do not overbeat. Gently beat in the ¼ cup sugar, 2 tablespoons at a time, until all the sugar has been absorbed and the peaks have slightly softened, 1 to 2 minutes.

Add one-third of the egg-white mixture to the batter and, using a rubber spatula, gently turn the mixture over on itself a few times to incorporate the whites. Add the rest of the egg whites and incorporate gently, turning the mixture over and over with the spatula until no streaks of white remain; the batter should remain fluffy.

Pour the batter into the pan and gently shake from side to side to

🖐 Mom Tip
Because powdered sugar tends to clump, put 1 teaspoon of it in a sieve and, while holding the sieve several inches above the cake, sift the sugar over the cake.

distribute it evenly. Bake for 25 to 30 minutes, or until the top of the cake is firm but a toothpick or cake tester inserted into the center comes out with a few moist crumbs attached. Remove from the oven and cool on a rack for 30 minutes. Just before serving, sprinkle with the powdered sugar (see Mom Tip). Cut the cake into 8 or 10 wedges, and serve directly from the pan. Offer Raspberry Sauce, if you wish, on the side. Store leftovers, covered, in the refrigerator. This cake tastes best warm or at room temperature, but it is also good cold.

Chocolate Polenta Cake

Serves: 10–12 ⏱ Preparation time: 30 minutes 🔥 Baking time: 45–50 minutes ⟍ Special equipment: 8- or 9-inch springform pan (see Mom Tip 1, page 44) ♨ Rating: Not So Easy

I was initially hesitant to make this recipe, since cornmeal didn't seem to be a worthy partner for chocolate. But the cake doesn't taste like corn at all. The cornmeal just smoothes out the chocolate a bit. I originally made this cake for Thanksgiving, which is a perfect occasion for it. The cake is formal enough so it won't seem out of place, but not so rich that everyone can't manage an extra slice on top of the turkey and stuffing.

6 squares (6 ounces) semisweet chocolate
¾ cup (1½ sticks) unsalted butter + more for greasing

☞ Mom Tip
Cornmeal comes in
yellow or white vari-
eties and is available
in boxes near the
flour. You can use
either.

1 teaspoon all-purpose flour + 1 teaspoon for dusting pan

4 large eggs

3 tablespoons slivered or sliced almonds, finely chopped

½ cup brown sugar

1 teaspoon vanilla extract

2 tablespoons cornmeal (see Mom Tip)

2 tablespoons sugar

½ teaspoon powdered sugar

Melt the chocolate and butter in a heavy frying pan over very low heat, stirring occasionally. When the chocolate is almost melted, turn off the heat and set aside to cool. The heat of the pan will melt the remaining chocolate.

Place an oven rack in the middle position and preheat the oven to 350°. Lightly rub the bottom and sides of an 8- or 9-inch springform pan with butter. Add the teaspoon of flour and swirl to coat the buttered surfaces. To make it easier to remove the cake from the pan, cut a piece of wax paper to fit the bottom of the pan. Place it in the pan and wipe it with a bit of butter. Set aside.

Separate the eggs, putting the yolks in a small cup and the whites in a large metal or ceramic bowl with no traces of grease. Set aside.

Put the egg yolks, almonds, brown sugar and vanilla in a food processor or a large bowl. Process, or beat with an electric mixer until well blended. Add the cooled chocolate mixture, and process or beat until well blended. Add the cornmeal and flour, and pulse or beat on low speed just until blended.

Beat the egg whites with the mixer just until they form stiff peaks.

Do not overbeat. Gently beat in the 2 tablespoons sugar until it has been absorbed and the peaks have slightly softened, 1 to 2 minutes.

Add one-third of the egg-white mixture to the batter and, using a rubber spatula, gently turn the mixture over on itself a few times to incorporate the whites. Add the rest of the egg whites and incorporate gently, turning the mixture over and over with the spatula until no streaks of white remain; the batter should remain fluffy.

Pour the batter into the pan and shake it from side to side several times to spread to all corners. Bake for 45 to 50 minutes, or until the top is firm and a toothpick or cake tester inserted into the center comes out with just a few crumbs sticking to it. Remove from the oven and cool on a rack for 10 minutes.

Loosen the cake by sliding a knife around the edges. Place the rack on top of the cake and turn the springform pan and rack over together. Remove the wax paper from the bottom of the cake. Lay a plate on the bottom of the cake and, holding the plate and the rack together, turn the cake right side up. Let it cool to room temperature (see Mom Warning). The cake will be about 1 inch thick.

Serve the cake cold or at room temperature. Just before serving, sprinkle the powdered sugar over the top, using a sieve. Store in an airtight container or wrapped in foil or plastic wrap.

Flourless Chocolate Mocha Cake

Serves: 16–24 ◔ Preparation time: 20 minutes ◉ Baking time: 45–60 minutes ◍ Chilling time: 4 hours ◊ Special equipment: 9- or 10-inch springform pan (see Mom Tip 1) ◈ Rating: Easy

☞ Mom Tip 1
A springform pan is a deep, round pan, 8, 9 or 10 inches in diameter, with a bottom that can be detached from the sides. It's very useful for untraditional cakes that aren't firm enough to be tipped out of the pan. Springform pans are available at cookware shops and cost between $10 and $12.

This cake is decadence: ten eggs, a pound of butter and a pound and a half of chocolate. Baking it may make you feel like Henry VIII's chef—except Henry wouldn't share it with fifteen of his friends.

12 squares (12 ounces) bittersweet chocolate
12 squares (12 ounces) unsweetened chocolate
2 cups (4 sticks) unsalted butter + more for greasing
2 teaspoons unsweetened cocoa powder for dusting pan (see Mom Tip 1)
2 cups sugar
10 large eggs
1 cup brewed coffee or 2 teaspoons instant coffee granules dissolved in 1 cup hot water
2 teaspoons vanilla extract
2 cups strawberries or raspberries (optional)

Melt both kinds of chocolate and the butter in a heavy frying pan over very low heat, stirring occasionally. When the chocolate is almost melted, turn off the heat and set aside to cool. The heat of the pan will melt the remaining chocolate.

Place an oven rack in the middle position and preheat the oven to 350°. Lightly rub the bottom and sides of a 9- or 10-inch springform pan with butter. Then swirl the cocoa around the pan. Wrap a large square of aluminum foil around the outside bottom of the pan in case the batter leaks.

Put the sugar and eggs in a food processor or a large bowl. Process, or beat with an electric mixer on high speed for about 2 minutes until pale yellow and frothy. Add the coffee and vanilla, and process, or beat on low speed for a few seconds, or until incorporated. Add the chocolate mixture, and process or beat on low speed until well blended.

Pour the batter into the pan. Bake for 45 to 60 minutes, or until the top begins to form a light crust and a toothpick or cake tester inserted into the center comes out clean. Remove from the oven and cool on a rack for about 30 minutes, or until the cake reaches room temperature. Cover the pan with foil or plastic wrap and refrigerate for at least 4 hours. Serve cold.

If you are using strawberries or raspberries, rinse them in cold water, drain them thoroughly, pat them dry with paper towels and set aside.

To serve, remove the sides of the springform pan and set the cake, still sitting on the bottom of the pan, on a serving platter. Arrange the strawberries or raspberries, if using, around the cake. Cut the cake into small slices. Store leftovers, covered, in the refrigerator.

Chocolate Pound Cake

Serves: 10–12 🕐 Preparation time: 30 minutes 🌡 Baking time: 40–45 minutes ✋ Chilling time: 1 hour 🗡 Special equipment: 6-cup tube pan (see Mom Tip 1) 👍 Rating: Easy

Mom Tip 1
A tube pan, which has a large hole in the center, cooks cakes more quickly than does a regular cake pan. Because of the hole, the heat reaches both sides of the cake as it bakes. Some tube pans have the number of cups they hold embossed on the metal. If yours doesn't, fill it with cups of water to judge the volume.

This recipe uses a tube pan, which makes the cake look like a giant Life Saver. The challenge of using a tube pan is getting the cake out of it in a perfect circle. If it starts to fall apart, give everyone a fork and let them hover over the pan like lions over a wounded elk.

1 cup (2 sticks) unsalted butter, softened to room temperature, + more for greasing

1½ cups flour + 1 teaspoon for dusting the pan

1 cup sugar

4 large eggs

1½ teaspoons vanilla extract

2 tablespoons brewed coffee or 1 teaspoon instant coffee granules dissolved in 2 tablespoons hot water

½ cup unsweetened cocoa powder

¾ teaspoon baking powder

🍮 Mom Tip 2
Getting the cake out
of a tube pan can be
tricky. For a smooth
getaway, be sure to
generously grease and
flour the pan before
putting in the batter.

½ teaspoon salt

½ cup semisweeet chocolate chips (optional)

1 pint fresh strawberries or raspberries (optional)

1 teaspoon powdered sugar (optional)

Place an oven rack in the middle position and preheat the oven to 325°. Generously rub the bottom and sides of a 6-cup tube pan with butter. Add the 1 teaspoon flour and swirl it around, coating the buttered surfaces (see Mom Tip 2).

Put the butter and sugar in a food processor or a large bowl. Process, or beat with an electric mixer until smooth and creamy. Add the eggs, vanilla and coffee, and beat on low speed until well incorporated. Add the flour, cocoa, baking powder and salt, and process, or beat on low speed just until blended. Do not beat the batter too much, or the cake will be tough. Stir in the chocolate chips, if using, by hand and mix thoroughly. Pour the batter into the pan. It will be very thick, so you will need to spread it out evenly with a knife or rubber spatula.

Bake for 40 to 45 minutes, or until the cake pulls away from the sides of the pan and a cake tester or knife inserted in the cake comes out clean. Remove from the oven and cool on a rack for 10 minutes.

If you are using strawberries or raspberries, rinse them in cold water, drain them thoroughly, pat them dry with paper towels and set aside.

Loosen the cake by sliding a knife around the edges of the pan. Place the rack on top of the cake and turn the cake pan and rack over together. If the cake won't come out, turn the pan back over and insert a plastic or rubber spatula between the outer edge of the cake and the pan and gently rock it back and forth until the cake loosens (see Mom

Tip 3). Remove the cake from the pan, as described. Then lay a plate on the bottom of the cake and, holding the plate and the rack together, turn the cake right side up. Let it cool to room temperature on the rack.

Transfer the cake to a serving plate. For decoration, if desired, sprinkle the powdered sugar over the top using a sieve. Arrange the strawberries or raspberries, if using, around the edges or piled in the center. Store the cake in an airtight container or wrapped in foil or plastic. Store any leftover fruit separately.

Four-Layer Buttermilk Chocolate Cake

Serves: 12–16 Ⓠ Preparation time: 40 minutes + 10–15 minutes for the icing 🕯 Baking time: 40–45 minutes ♨ Rating: Not So Easy

*S*licing horizontally through this cake to make the layers can be a challenge. But if the Egyptians could build the Pyramids without cranes, you can build a four-layer cake. The labor is worth it: it's four times the cake in every bite.

> ¾ cup (1½ sticks) unsalted butter, softened to room temperature, + more for greasing
>
> 2 cups all-purpose flour + 1 teaspoon for dusting
>
> 4 squares (4 ounces) unsweetened chocolate

🖑 Mom Tip 1
Buttermilk is available
in cartons near the
regular milk.

1 cup sugar

1 cup brown sugar

3 large eggs

2 teaspoons vanilla extract

2 cups buttermilk (see Mom Tip 1)

2 teaspoons baking soda

½ teaspoon salt

1½–2 cups Chocolate Buttercream Icing (page 68) or
  Couldn't-Be-Simpler Chocolate Icing (page 65);
  also, see Mom Tip 2

Place an oven rack in the middle position and preheat the oven to 350°. Lightly rub the bottom and sides of a 9-x-13-inch cake pan with butter. Add the 1 teaspoon flour and swirl it around to coat. To make it easier to remove the cake from the pan, cut a piece of wax paper to fit the bottom of the pan. Place it in the pan and wipe it with a bit of butter. Set aside.

Melt the chocolate in a small, heavy pot over very low heat, stirring constantly. When the chocolate is almost melted, turn off the heat and set aside to cool. The heat of the pot will melt the remaining chocolate.

Put the butter and sugars in a food processor or a large bowl. Process, or beat with an electric mixer until smooth and creamy. Add the eggs, vanilla and melted chocolate, and process, or beat on low speed until well blended. Add half the buttermilk, and process, or beat on low speed until blended. Add the flour, baking soda and salt, and pulse or beat on low speed just until blended. Add the remaining buttermilk, and pulse or beat just until blended. Do not overmix, or the cake will be tough.

Pour the batter into the pan and shake it from side to side several times so the batter spreads to all corners. Bake for 40 to 45 minutes, or until the cake pulls away from the sides of the pan and a cake tester or knife inserted into the center comes out clean. Remove from the oven and cool for 10 minutes. Loosen the cake by sliding a knife around the edges of the pan. Place a cooling rack over the top of the cake and, with a pot holder in each hand, carefully turn over the rack and cake pan. The cake should slip out of the pan. If it doesn't, hit it on the bottom with the flat of your hand. Let the cake cool to room temperature while upside down. Remove the wax paper from the bottom of the cake.

Cut the cake in half so that you have two rectangles, 9 by 6 or 6½ inches. Using a serrated bread knife or other long knife, carefully slice horizontally through the center of each cake, making 2 separate layers.

Slide a large, flat item such as a pizza paddle, a rimless cookie sheet or a large piece of cardboard between the layers of the first rectangle. Transfer the top layer to a serving platter.

Spread a thin layer of icing over the top with a wide-bladed knife. Place the bottom of the first rectangle on top of the icing, lining the edges up. Spread some icing over this layer. Transfer the top layer of the second rectangle temporarily to a plate; set aside. Place the bottom of the second rectangle on top of the iced layer. Line up the edges and spread some icing over this third layer. Place the reserved layer on the top and line up the edges.

Gently spread some icing over the top of the cake, making sure not to dislodge any cake crumbs. Ice the sides. Spread any leftover icing on top of the cake. Serve cold or at room temperature. Store in an airtight container or wrapped in foil or plastic wrap.

Early 1600s The word begins to spread to the rest of Europe about chocolate. Spanish monks and friars, who are largely responsible for its manufacture, share the new beverage with visitors from France, Italy and beyond. Since European desserts usually consist mostly of nut loaf and blancmange, chocolate is an instant underground hit. Monks across Europe attend chocolate raves.

You-Deserve-It Fudge Cake

Serves: 10–12 Preparation time: 20 minutes Baking time: 30–35 minutes Rating: Easy

Mom Tip 1
Instead of brandy, you can substitute whiskey or a liqueur such as Kahlúa or Cointreau. Or use 3 tablespoons cold coffee and 1 teaspoon vanilla extract. Alcohol or vanilla extract, which contains a high percentage of alcohol, intensifies the flavor of chocolate.

Fudge is a magic word, calling to mind the ultimate chocolate rush. This cake lives up to its name. It has no nuts, no icing, no crust—nothing to get between you and your chocolate.

- 12 squares (12 ounces) bittersweet or semisweet chocolate or one 12-ounce bag semisweet chocolate chips
- ⅓ cup slivered or sliced almonds
- ½ cup (1 stick) unsalted butter, softened to room temperature, + more for greasing
- ¾ cup all-purpose flour + 1 teaspoon for dusting
- 3 large eggs
- ¼ cup sugar + ¼ cup sugar
- 3 tablespoons brandy (see Mom Tip 1)
- 1 teaspoon instant coffee granules

Powdered sugar (optional)
Fresh raspberries (optional)

Melt the chocolate in a heavy frying pan over very low heat, stirring constantly. When the chocolate is almost melted, turn off the heat and set aside to cool. The heat of the pan will melt the remaining chocolate.

Place an oven rack in the middle position and preheat the oven to 350°.

Spread the slivered almonds on a cookie sheet and bake for about 5 minutes, or until they begin to turn golden brown. Be careful they don't burn. Remove from the oven and, when cool, grind them in a food processor or blender or chop by hand. Set aside.

Lightly rub the bottom and sides of a 9-x-5-inch bread pan with butter. Add the teaspoon of flour and swirl to coat the buttered surfaces. Cut a piece of wax paper to fit the bottom of the pan. Place it in the pan, and wipe it with butter. Set aside.

Separate the eggs, putting the yolks in a small cup and the whites in a medium metal or ceramic bowl with no traces of grease. Set aside.

Put the butter and ¼ cup sugar in a food processor or a large bowl. Process, or beat with an electric mixer until smooth and creamy. Add the egg yolks, and process, or beat on low speed until well blended. Add the cooled chocolate, and process or beat until blended. Combine the brandy and coffee granules in a small cup, and stir until the granules dissolve. Add to the batter, and pulse, or beat on low speed until well blended. Add the almonds and flour, and process, or beat on low speed just until blended. Do not beat the batter too much, or the cake will be tough.

Mom Tip 2
The beaten egg whites lighten the batter. Don't stir so hard that they lose their fluffiness.

Beat the egg whites with the mixer just until they form stiff peaks. Do not overbeat. Gently beat in the other ¼ cup sugar, 2 tablespoons at a time, until all the sugar has been absorbed and the peaks have slightly softened, 1 to 2 minutes.

Add one-third of the egg-white mixture to the batter and, using a rubber spatula, gently turn the mixture over on itself a few times to incorporate the whites. Add the rest of the egg whites and incorporate gently, turning the batter over and over until no streaks of white remain (see Mom Tip 2).

Pour the batter into the pan and gently shake from side to side so the batter spreads to all corners. Bake for 30 to 35 minutes, or until the top is firm and a toothpick or cake tester inserted into the center comes out with a few moist crumbs attached.

Remove from the oven and cool on a rack for 10 minutes. Loosen the cake by sliding a knife around the edges of the pan. Place the rack on top of the cake and, with a pot holder in each hand, turn the cake pan and rack over together. If the cake won't come out, turn the pan back over and insert a plastic or rubber spatula between the outer edge of the cake and the pan and gently rock it back and forth until the cake loosens. Remove the wax paper from the bottom of the cake. Turn the cake right side up and let it cool to room temperature on the rack. Serve cold or at room temperature.

Just before serving, transfer the cake to a serving plate and, if you like, sprinkle with the powdered sugar, using a sieve. Slice thinly at the table and serve with the fresh raspberries on the side, if desired. Store in an airtight container or wrapped in foil or plastic wrap.

Devil's Food Cake

Serves: 12 ⓧ Preparation time: 20 minutes + 10–15 minutes for the icing 🕯 Baking time: 25–35 minutes ⚖ Rating: Easy

I don't know what heavenly matters have to do with chocolate, but I'll bet that Satan has the best. I'll take Devil's Food Cake over Angel Food Cake any day.

¾ cup (1½ sticks) unsalted butter, softened to room temperature, + more for greasing
2 cups all-purpose flour + 2 teaspoons for dusting pans

🐦 Mom Tip 1
Combining boiling
water and cocoa
brings out the most
intense chocolate
flavor.

🐦 Mom Tip 2
If you prefer a sheet
cake, bake the cake in
one 9-x-13-inch pan
for 40 to 45 minutes.

1⅓ cups boiling water (see Mom Tip 1)
¾ cup unsweetened cocoa powder
1¾ cups sugar
2 large eggs
1 teaspoon vanilla extract
1¼ teaspoons baking soda
½ teaspoon salt
1½–2 cups Chocolate Buttercream Icing (page 68) or
Couldn't-Be-Simpler Chocolate Icing (page 65)

Place an oven rack in the middle position and preheat the oven to 350°.
Lightly rub the bottom and sides of two 8- or 9-inch cake pans (see
Mom Tip 2) with butter. Add 1 teaspoon flour to each pan and swirl it
around, coating the buttered surfaces. To make it easier to remove the
cakes from the pans, cut a piece of wax paper to fit the bottom of each
pan. Place them in the pans and wipe them with a bit of butter. Set aside.

In a bowl, stir together the boiling water and cocoa. Set aside to cool.

Put the butter and sugar in a food processor or a large bowl. Process,
or beat with an electric mixer until smooth and creamy. Add the eggs
and vanilla, and process, or beat with an electric mixer on low speed
until well blended. Add half the cocoa mixture, and pulse or beat until
blended. Add the flour, baking soda and salt, and process, or beat on
low speed just until blended. Add the remaining cocoa mixture, and
pulse again or beat just until blended. Do not beat the batter too much,
or the cake will be tough.

Pour the batter into the pans and shake them from side to side several times so the batter spreads to all corners. Bake on the middle rack

—at least 2 inches apart—for 30 to 35 minutes (for 8-inch pans) or 25 to 30 minutes (for 9-inch pans), or until the cake pulls away from the sides of the pan and a cake tester or knife inserted into the center comes out clean. Remove from the oven and cool for 10 minutes.

Loosen the cakes by sliding a knife around the edges of each pan. Place cooling racks over the top of each cake layer and, with a pot holder in each hand, carefully turn over the racks and cake pans. The cakes should slip out onto the racks. If they don't, hit them on the bottom with the flat of your hand. Let the cakes cool to room temperature upside down. Remove the wax paper from the bottom of each cake.

To ice the cake, put one layer, bottom side up, on a large plate or tray and spread some icing over the top with a wide-bladed knife. At this point, don't ice the sides. Carefully place the second layer, bottom side down, on top of the first layer. Spread some icing over the top layer, making sure not to press so hard that cake crumbs are dislodged into the icing. Then ice the sides. Spread any leftover icing on top of the cake. Serve cold or at room temperature. Store in an airtight container or wrapped in foil or plastic wrap.

Sachertorte

Serves: 10–12 ☼ Preparation time: 30 minutes + 10 minutes for the glaze 🔥 Baking time: 20–25 minutes ✋ Chilling time: 30 minutes 👍 Rating: Not So Easy

~~~~~~

Bakeries are full of elaborate cakes with edible flowers and other look-at-me features. But a lot of them taste like sweetened sawdust. Sachertorte is a moist chocolate cake with a layer of apricot jam and a chocolate glaze. It doesn't come with a free balloon, but it sure tastes good.

> ¾ cup (1 ½ sticks) unsalted butter, softened to room temperature, + more for greasing
> 1 ¾ cups all-purpose flour + 2 teaspoons for dusting
> 6 squares (6 ounces) semisweet chocolate
> 6 large eggs
> ½ cup sugar + ¼ cup sugar
> 1 teaspoon vanilla extract

1–1½ cups apricot jam
    1 cup Easy Chocolate Glaze (page 66)

Place an oven rack in the middle position and preheat the oven to 300°.

Lightly rub the bottom and sides of two 8- or 9-inch cake pans with butter. Add 1 teaspoon flour to each pan and swirl it around, coating the buttered surfaces. To make it easier to remove the cakes from the pans, cut a piece of wax paper to fit the bottom of each pan. Place them in the pans and wipe them with a bit of butter. Set aside.

Melt the chocolate in a small, heavy pot over very low heat, stirring constantly. When it's almost melted, turn off the heat and set aside to cool. The heat of the pot will melt the remaining chocolate.

Separate the eggs, putting the yolks in a small cup and the whites in a large metal or ceramic bowl with no traces of grease. Set aside.

Put the butter and the ½ cup sugar in a food processor or a large bowl. Process, or beat with an electric mixer on high speed until smooth and creamy. Add the egg yolks and pulse until incorporated. Add the vanilla and melted chocolate, and process or beat on low speed until well blended. Add the flour, and process or beat on low speed just until blended. Do not beat the batter too much, or the cake will be tough.

Beat the egg whites with the mixer just until they form stiff peaks. Do not overbeat. Gently beat in the ¼ cup sugar, 2 tablespoons at a time, until all the sugar has been absorbed and the peaks have slightly softened, 1 to 2 minutes.

Add one-third of the egg-white mixture to the batter and, using a rubber spatula, gently turn the mixture over on itself a few times to incorporate the whites. Add the rest of the egg whites and incorporate

Mom Tip
If you want to write something on the cake, save a few table-spoons of glaze. Once the cake is iced, put some of the glaze on a spoon and dribble letters onto the cake. Or put the glaze in a small plastic storage bag, snip off about ⅛ inch of one corner and squeeze out the glaze as you write. If the glaze seems too thick, reheat it over low heat. If it's still too thick, add 1 to 2 drops of milk or cream, and stir. If you mess up the writing, don't worry—you can pretend it's a decoration.

gently, turning the mixture over and over with the spatula until no streaks of white remain; the batter should remain fluffy.

Pour the batter into the pans and shake them from side to side several times so the batter spreads to the edges. Bake on the middle rack—at least 2 inches apart from each other—for 20 to 25 minutes, or until the cake pulls away from the sides of the pan and a cake tester or knife inserted into the center comes out clean. Remove from the oven and cool for 10 minutes. Loosen the cake by sliding a knife around the edges of each pan. Place cooling racks over the top of each pan and, with a pot holder in each hand, carefully turn over the racks and cake pans. The cakes should slip out of the pans onto the racks. Let them cool to room temperature while upside down. Remove the wax paper from the bottom of each cake.

Put 1 cup of the apricot jam in a small pot and begin heating over medium-high heat, stirring constantly, until it softens and begins to bubble around the edges, about 1 minute. If the jam has large pieces of fruit in it, remove them before spreading the jam on the cake. To do this, spoon about ½ cup hot jam into a small sieve and, holding the sieve over a small bowl, press the jam through the sieve with a spoon. Continue this process until all the heated jam has been sieved. Discard the fruit pieces left in the sieve or save for another use.

Put 1 cake layer, bottom side up, on a large plate or tray. Spread about ½ cup of the jam with a spoon or knife, making sure the jam completely covers the top but not the sides. Add a little remaining jam, if necessary. Carefully place the second layer, bottom side down, on top of the first layer. Spread the rest of the heated jam over the top layer. If there's not enough, heat another ½ cup as described.

Refrigerate the cake, uncovered, for 30 minutes, to firm up the jam.

To ICE THE CAKE: Spread some chocolate glaze over the apricot jam with a wide-bladed knife, making sure not to press so hard that the jam is dislodged and mixed in with the icing. Make the glaze as smooth as possible. Spread the rest on the sides of the cake (see Mom Tip). Refrigerate, uncovered, for about 30 minutes, or until the glaze has set. Then, cover the cake until needed. Serve cold or at room temperature. Store in an airtight container or wrapped in foil or plastic wrap.

Marble Cheesecake

Serves: 10–12 ☼ Preparation time: 30 minutes + 10 minutes for the icing 🔥 Baking time: 50–60 minutes ✋ Chilling time: 4½ hours ✎ Special equipment: 8- or 9-inch springform pan (see Mom Tip 1, page 44) ✎ Rating: Not So Easy

After several decades of watching Mom make her own birthday cake, I told her I'd make her any cake she wanted for her next birthday. She chose this one, a decadent cheesecake with a groovy chocolate-vanilla swirl. It was so filling she could hardly eat the chocolate she got for her birthday present.

- 1½ cups chocolate graham cracker crumbs (about one-third of a 16-ounce package)
- ¼ cup (½ stick) unsalted butter + more for greasing
- 3 squares (3 ounces) semisweet chocolate
- 3 8-ounce packages cream cheese, softened to room temperature
- ½ cup sugar

½ cup brown sugar
5 large eggs
1 teaspoon vanilla extract
¼ cup semisweet chocolate chips
    Couldn't-Be-Simpler Chocolate Icing (page 65)
    Fresh strawberries or raspberries (optional)

Place an oven rack in the middle position and preheat the oven to 325°.

TO MAKE THE CRUST: Grind the graham crackers into fine crumbs in a food processor or blender, or put them in a plastic bag and crush them with a rolling pin or heavy can. You should have about 1½ cups crumbs.

Melt the butter in a small, heavy pot over low heat. Add to the crumbs and mix thoroughly.

Lightly rub the bottom and sides of an 8- or 9-inch springform pan with butter. Scrape the crumb mixture into the springform pan. With your hands, press the crumbs firmly and evenly into the bottom of the pan and about 1 inch up the sides. Set aside.

Melt the chocolate in a small, heavy pot over very low heat, stirring constantly. When it is almost melted, turn off the heat and set aside to cool. The heat of the pot will melt the remaining chocolate.

Put the cream cheese, the sugars, eggs and vanilla in a large bowl. Beat for about 2 minutes with an electric mixer or about 5 minutes with a wooden spoon, until the mixture is smooth. Spoon about half the mixture over the crust. Add the melted chocolate to the remaining mixture and beat on low speed for about 10 seconds, or until thoroughly mixed. Stir in the chocolate chips.

Pour the chocolate batter on top of the white batter and drag a knife

 Mom Tip
Don't worry about
any cracks that may
develop in the center
of the cheesecake.
The topping will
cover them.

through the two batters to give a swirled effect. Bake for 50 to 60 minutes, or until the top begins to brown. The center may seem a bit wobbly, but it will become firm as it cools. Remove from the oven and cool on a rack for about 30 minutes (see Mom Tip).

When the cake reaches room temperature, remove the sides of the springform pan and set the cheesecake, still on the bottom of the pan, on a serving platter. Spread the icing over the top and sides of the cake. Refrigerate, uncovered, for about 30 minutes, or until the icing has set. Then cover the cheesecake with foil or plastic wrap and refrigerate for at least 4 hours. Serve cold, with fresh strawberries or raspberries on the side, if desired. Store leftovers, covered, in the refrigerator.

Couldn't-Be-Simpler Chocolate Icing

Makes: About 2 cups (enough for a 2-layer cake or a 9-x-13-inch sheet cake) ⏱ Preparation time: 10 minutes ✋ Rating: Very Easy

Chocolate and sour cream. That's it. And it tastes good. Don't ask any questions.

2 cups (12-ounce package) semisweet chocolate chips
1 cup light sour cream (see Mom Tip)

Mom Tip
Use light sour cream —to me, it tastes just as good when mixed with chocolate as regular sour cream, and it has less fat.

Melt the chocolate chips in a heavy frying pan over very low heat, stirring constantly. When the chocolate is almost melted, turn off the heat and set aside to cool. The heat of the pan will melt the remaining chocolate.

When the chocolate is fully melted, add the sour cream and stir until smooth. Work quickly with this icing, because it hardens as it reaches room temperature.

1615 Chocolate reaches France. Fourteen-year-old Anne of Austria (who was actually from Spain — go figure) enters into an arranged marriage with the similarly pubescent Louis XIII of France. Nervous about coming directly to the throne from the Girl Scouts, she brings along chocolate to make herself feel more at home. The young king doesn't care for the new drink — or his new wife, for that matter — but the chocolate beverage soon becomes the "in" drink at the French court.

Easy Chocolate Glaze

Makes: About 1 cup (enough to pour over the top of any size cake) ⏱ Preparation time: 10 minutes
👍 Rating: Very Easy

What's the difference between "glaze" and "icing"? Glaze is thinner and glossier. Think of glaze as a windbreaker, while icing is a wool coat.

> 1 cup (6-ounce package) semisweet chocolate chips
> 2 tablespoons unsalted butter
> 2 tablespoons light corn syrup
> 2 tablespoons milk
> ½ teaspoon vanilla extract

The glaze needs to be warm and runny to be spread. To use leftover glaze, heat the container in a pan partly filled with hot water; don't let any of the water get into the chocolate. Stir the mixture until it becomes spreadable.

Melt the chocolate chips and butter in a small, heavy pot over very low heat, stirring constantly. When the chocolate is almost melted, turn off the heat and set aside to cool. The heat of the pot will melt the remaining chocolate.

When the chocolate is fully melted, add the corn syrup, milk and vanilla, and stir until smooth. Use while still warm. Store any leftover glaze in the refrigerator in a covered container (see Mom Tip).

1624 **The practice of monks consuming chocolate is called into question. In Vienna, Joan Franc Rauch publishes a tract calling chocolate a violent inflamer of the passions and demanding that monks be forbidden from drinking the beverage. The monks resist. They've already taken a vow of chastity—they aren't about to give up chocolate, too.**

Chocolate Buttercream Icing

Makes: about 2 cups (enough for a 2-layer cake or a 9-x-13-inch sheet cake) Preparation time: 5 minutes (using a food processor) or 10 minutes (by hand) Rating: Very Easy

For years I've enjoyed buttercream icing on my birthday cakes. But the fact that the icing wasn't chocolate did cause some inner conflict. My mom resolved the crisis by making a chocolate version. I've reached an age where I no longer look forward to birthdays, but this icing on the cake softens the blow.

Mom Tip
To make Chocolate Mint Buttercream Icing, add ½ teaspoon peppermint extract when you add the vanilla.

- ½ cup (1 stick) unsalted butter, softened to room temperature
- 1 16-ounce box powdered sugar
- ¼ cup unsweetened cocoa powder
- ⅛ teaspoon salt
- 1 teaspoon vanilla extract (see Mom Tip)
- 2 tablespoons sour cream or plain yogurt + more if needed

✸✷! Mom Warning
The icing should be
thin enough to spread
easily but not so thin
that it's runny. How-
ever, if it's too thick,
crumbs of cake will
loosen and stick to it
when you try to
spread it. The ideal
consistency is like that
of mayonnaise. Icing
will dry slightly after
it's spread on the
cake. If you inadver-
tently get crumbs
mixed in with the
icing, just pretend it's
decoration.

Put the butter in a food processor or a large bowl. Process, or beat with an electric mixer until smooth. Add the powdered sugar, cocoa, salt and vanilla, and process or beat until well blended. The mixture will be very thick. Add 2 tablespoons sour cream or yogurt, and process or beat until smooth. This may thin the icing enough to make it spreadable, but you may need more to get the right consistency (see Mom Warning).

Use immediately.

Ganache

Makes: About 1½ cups ☾ Preparation time: 15 minutes ✋ Rating: Very Easy

~~~~~~

Ganache is a creamy French chocolate mixture used for topping or as the basis for truffles. Spoon it on ice cream or fruit, or straight into your mouth. It was reportedly invented when an apprentice chocolate-maker accidentally spilled hot milk into some chocolate. The master, thinking his slow-witted assistant had ruined the chocolate, called him a *ganache*, the French word for "imbecile." He mixed the chocolate concoction in hopes of saving it, and ganache was born. I wonder if the French at first hesitated to eat this new delicacy; I know I'd think twice if someone offered me a plate of "moron."

    8 squares (8 ounces) bittersweet or semisweet chocolate
    1 cup heavy cream

Mom Tip
If the ganache isn't thick enough to spread, transfer it to the bowl of an electric mixer and beat it for several minutes, or beat it by hand with a wooden spoon.

Melt the chocolate in a heavy frying pan over very low heat, stirring constantly. When the chocolate is almost melted, turn off the heat and set aside to cool. The heat of the pan will melt the remaining chocolate.

Stir in the cream and mix thoroughly. If the chocolate separates into flecks, resume heating over very low heat for about 30 seconds, or until the mixture warms up enough for the chocolate to blend into the cream. Remove from the heat.

To use ganache as a glaze for a cake, pour it over the cake while the ganache is still warm. To use it as an icing, let it cool to room temperature and it will thicken enough to spread (see Mom Tip). Refrigerate any unused ganache. It will keep for about 1 week.

Quick Fudge Icing

Makes: About 1 cup (enough for a 9-x-13-inch cake or 48 cookies) ⏲ Preparation time: 10 minutes
✋ Cooling time: 15 minutes ⚖ Rating: Very Easy

I used to buy cans of chocolate frosting and just dive in with a spoon. Somehow it seems more sophisticated when I eat this icing right out of the pan. And sometimes when I'm feeling really, really sophisticated, I actually spread this icing on a cake.

    8 squares (8 ounces) semisweet chocolate
    ½ cup heavy cream
    1 tablespoon light corn syrup
    1 tablespoon brown sugar (see Mom Tip)
    2 tablespoons unsalted butter
    ½ teaspoon vanilla extract

Mom Tip
For a slightly different
taste, substitute
honey or maple syrup
for the brown sugar.

Melt the chocolate in a heavy frying pan over very low heat, stirring constantly. When the chocolate is almost melted, add the cream, corn syrup and brown sugar and stir to combine. Increase the heat to medium and bring the mixture to a boil, stirring constantly. Remove from the heat and add the butter and vanilla. Set aside to cool, stirring occasionally until the butter has melted.

When the mixture has reached room temperature (about 15 minutes), it is ready for use. If it seems too runny, refrigerate for 15 minutes before spreading it.

Cookies/
Brownies

ookies and brownies are the finger foods of the chocolate family. Not only can they hold just as much chocolate power per bite as the bigger desserts, but they have the advantage of being snacks. After all, if you bake a cake for dessert, you can't simply eat a slice two hours before dinner. But with cookies and brownies, no one will know if you pilfer a couple.

Brownie Cookies ★ 76

Chocolate Butter Cookies ★ 78

Chocolate Coconut Macaroons ★ 80

Chocolate Thumbprints ★ 82

Lava Cookies ★ 84

Spicy Chocolate Cookies ★ 86

Chocolate Shortbread Cookies ★ 88

Florentines ★ 90

Traditional Chocolate Chip Cookies ★ 93

Positively Sinful Chocolate Chip
     Meringues ★ 96

Chocolate Chip Peanut Butter Cookies ★ 99

Chocolate-Dipped Biscotti ★ 102

Double-Sided Double Chocolate Chip
     Cookies ★ 105

Triple Chocolate Brownies ★ 108

Movie Star Brownies ★ 110

Congo Bars ★ 112

Intensely Chocolate Cocoa Brownies ★ 114

Chocolate Oatmeal Brownies ★ 116

Peanut Butter Chocolate Brownies ★ 118

Brownie Macaroons ★ 120

Chocolate-Lovers' Lemon Squares ★ 122

Chocolate Turtle Bars ★ 125

Jaffa Squares ★ 128

Blondies Topped with Chocolate and
     Nuts ★ 130

Chocolate Crispy Rice Treats ★ 132

No-Bake Chocolate Granola Bars ★ 134

1660s Samuel Pepys, famous diarist and chronicler of Reformation-era English life, makes chocolate part of his daily routine. Between dodging flames in the Great London Fire and holding his breath so as not to catch the plague, Pepys consumes large amounts of what he calls "jocolatte." His spelling may be questionable, and his pursuit of the family maid even more so, but his passion for the new drink indicates that chocolate is making inroads into English society.

Brownie Cookies

Makes: 36 cookies ⏲ Preparation time: 20 minutes 🕯 Baking time: 24–30 minutes (8–10 minutes per batch) 🖐 Rating: Easy

I've always loved to eat cookie dough. I rarely get as far as putting the cookies in the oven: I just sit on the couch and eat right out of the bowl. But now I'm married to a doctor, and she disapproves of my eating anything with raw eggs in it. I figure if Rocky Balboa can drink a whole glass of raw eggs, I can sneak a few mouthfuls of cookie batter when she's not looking. Brownie Cookies have the best dough. And thanks to my wife's supervision, I now know the cookies themselves taste just as good.

   5 tablespoons unsalted butter + more for greasing
   8 squares (8 ounces) bittersweet chocolate
   1 cup sugar
   3 large eggs

1 teaspoon vanilla extract
½ cup all-purpose flour
½ teaspoon baking powder
¼ teaspoon salt
1 cup (6-ounce package) semisweet chocolate chips
1 cup chopped walnuts

Place an oven rack in the middle position and preheat the oven to 350°. Lightly rub two cookie sheets with butter, or use nonstick baking sheets. Set aside.

Melt the chocolate and butter in a heavy pan over very low heat, stirring occasionally. When the chocolate is almost melted, turn off the heat and set aside. The heat of the pan will melt the remaining chocolate.

Put the sugar, eggs and vanilla in a large bowl. Beat with an electric mixer or a wooden spoon until pale yellow and frothy, about 2 minutes on high speed, or much longer by hand. Add the chocolate mixture and beat at low speed for about 15 seconds, or about 1 minute by hand, until thoroughly mixed. Add the flour, baking powder and salt and mix just until blended. Stir in the chocolate chips and nuts by hand and mix thoroughly.

Drop 12 tablespoonfuls of dough on each sheet, 3 cookies per row in 4 rows. Bake each batch, one sheet at a time, for 8 to 10 minutes. The cookies will have cracked and slightly flaky tops and be slightly soft. Remove from the oven and cool on the sheet for about 3 minutes (see Mom Tip). Transfer them with a spatula to a cooling rack. Let the first cookie sheet cool for 1 or 2 minutes more before reusing so the dough doesn't melt. Store the cookies in an airtight container.

1660s Male-only chocolate houses spring up all over England. Here respectable wealthy men can retreat from the daily grind of fox hunts and wig-fittings and relax with like-minded aristocrats. Safely behind closed doors, they casually discuss politics and other issues of the day and engage in the occasional wager. The ban against women is necessary: the men drink so much chocolate they are ashamed to let their wives see.

Chocolate Butter Cookies

Makes: 36 cookies 🕐 Preparation time: 30 minutes 🌱 Baking time: 15 minutes 🐌 Rating: Very Easy

These cookies are small enough to pop in your mouth one after another. They're like human "Scooby" snacks. It's tempting to keep stuffing them in, just to see how many will fit. When I was young, I used to amuse my sister by filling my mouth with seedless grapes. When thirty-five of them were packed in there, she would be laughing hysterically, and I would be unable to breathe. It's a miracle that I survived childhood—or have I?

   1 cup slivered or sliced almonds, chopped
   ½ cup (1 stick) unsalted butter, softened to room temperature
   3 tablespoons powdered sugar + more for optional
       decoration
   ⅔ cup all-purpose flour
   ¼ cup unsweetened cocoa powder

Place an oven rack in the middle position and preheat the oven to 325°.

Spread the almonds on a cookie sheet and bake for about 5 minutes, or until they begin to turn golden brown. Be careful they don't burn. Remove them from the oven and set aside until cool.

Put the butter and sugar in a food processor or a large bowl, and process, or beat with an electric mixer until smooth and creamy. Add the almonds, flour and cocoa, and pulse for about 10 seconds, or beat on low speed just until blended.

Set out a cookie sheet, but do not grease it. Shape the dough into ¾-inch balls and place them on the cookie sheet about ½ inch apart (see Mom Tip). The cookies will flatten out slightly as they bake.

Bake for about 15 minutes, or until they look firm but have not begun to brown. Remove from the oven and immediately transfer the cookies to a rack. When cool, transfer them to a plate. For decoration, sprinkle with a little powdered sugar, using a sieve. Store in an airtight container or wrapped in foil or plastic wrap.

Chocolate Coconut Macaroons

Makes: 36 cookies ⏰ Preparation time: 15 minutes 🔥 Cooking time: 22 minutes (11 minutes per batch) ✋ Rating: Very Easy

Since my mom is such a good cook, she often gets talked into bringing food to events. And sometimes, since I live close by, I get snookered into doing all the work. She recently asked me to make Chocolate Coconut Macaroons for a meeting she was attending at a small theater. The participants tried my coconut-flavored cookies before the meeting, and loved them. But while they were in the meeting, some actors snuck in and ate the rest. I guess it's a compliment when people steal your food.

Butter for greasing
6 squares (6 ounces) semisweet chocolate
2 squares (2 ounces) unsweetened chocolate
4 large egg whites
½ teaspoon cream of tartar

1⅓ cups sugar

2 teaspoons vanilla extract

4 cups sweetened shredded coconut

Place an oven rack in the middle position and preheat the oven to 325°. Lightly rub two cookie sheets with butter, or use nonstick baking sheets. Set aside.

Melt the two chocolates in a heavy frying pan over very low heat, stirring constantly. When the chocolate is almost melted, turn off the heat and set aside to cool. The heat of the pan will melt the remaining chocolate.

Put the egg whites in a large mixing bowl with no traces of grease. Beat with an electric mixer until the whites are foamy. Add the cream of tartar and continue beating just until they form stiff peaks. Do not over-beat. Gently beat in the sugar, 2 tablespoons at a time, until all the sugar has been absorbed and the peaks have slightly softened, 1 to 2 minutes.

Add the melted chocolate and vanilla and mix gently with a rubber spatula until no white streaks show. Then stir in the coconut, making sure it is completely incorporated, but take care not to deflate the batter by overmixing. Drop 18 teaspoonfuls of dough onto each cookie sheet, leaving at least 1 inch between each cookie. Bake each batch, one cookie sheet at a time, for about 11 minutes. The cookies will be firm to the touch and just beginning to brown. Remove from the oven and cool on the sheet for about 3 minutes. Then transfer them with a spatula to a cooling rack. Store in an airtight container.

Late 1600s Louis XIV, the historical figure most in need of an emergency makeover, builds his magnificent palace at Versailles and fills it with every luxury. From the Hall of Mirrors to the gold-plated chamber pots, no detail is too expensive for Louis to tax his people to build it. Louis's mistress, Madame de Maintenon, insists that chocolate be served at banquets, and he obliges her. Chocolate is very popular with his guests, and Louis continues to serve it long after he parts ways with Madame de Maintenon and moves on to a series of new mistresses.

Chocolate Thumbprints

Makes: 50–54 cookies Preparation time: 20 minutes Baking time: 36–45 minutes (12–15 minutes per batch) Rating: Not So Easy

Chocolate Thumbprints doesn't refer to the evidence you leave behind after a midnight binge. They're chocolate cookies with a thumb-made divot that you fill with melted chocolate. Hopefully, you have a big thumb.

        1 cup (2 sticks) unsalted butter, softened to room
            temperature
        ⅔ cup sugar
        1 large egg
        1 teaspoon vanilla extract
        2 cups all-purpose flour
        3 tablespoons unsweetened cocoa powder

¼ teaspoon salt

1 cup semisweet mini chocolate chips

1 cup (6-ounce package) semisweet chocolate chips

Place an oven rack in the middle position and preheat the oven to 350°. Set out two cookie sheets, but do not grease them.

Put the butter and sugar in a food processor or a large bowl. Process, or beat with an electric mixer until smooth and creamy. Add the egg and vanilla, and process or beat until well blended. Add the flour, cocoa, salt and mini chocolate chips, and pulse for about 10 seconds or beat on low speed just until blended. The dough will be very stiff.

Using a tablespoon as a guide, scoop a portion of dough and, with your hands, roll each portion into a ball. Place the balls on each sheet, 3 cookies per row in 6 rows. Put your thumb in the center of each ball and push to flatten, leaving a deep thumbprint. Bake each batch, one cookie sheet at a time, for 12 to 15 minutes. The cookies will be firm to the touch. Remove from the oven and cool on the sheet for about 3 minutes. Then transfer them with a spatula to a cooling rack. Let the cookie sheet cool for 1 or 2 minutes more before reusing so the dough doesn't melt.

Melt the semisweet chocolate chips in a small, heavy pot over very low heat, stirring constantly. When the chocolate is almost melted, turn off the heat and set aside to cool. The heat of the pot will melt the remaining chocolate. When the chocolate is fully melted, spoon a teaspoonful into each cookie thumbprint. Set the cookies aside to cool. Store in single layers, separated by wax paper, in an airtight container.

Lava Cookies

Makes: 36 cookies ⏱ Preparation time: 15 minutes 🖐 Chilling time: 15 minutes 🔥 Baking time: 30–36 minutes (10–12 minutes per batch) ✍ Rating: Easy

〜〜

I t's hard to name a newly created dish. I'm sure whoever invented pizza had a heck of a time coming up with a suitable name. The surface of these chocolate cookies looks like the dried, cracked remains of Pompeii after the eruption of Mount Vesuvius. Thus, "Lava Cookies." Why not? They don't taste like volcanic residue, but it's better than "Chocolate Cookie #78."

 3 squares (3 ounces) unsweetened chocolate
 6 tablespoons unsalted butter + more for greasing
 1 cup sugar
 2 large eggs
 1 teaspoon vanilla extract
 1 cup all-purpose flour

If you're not in a hurry
to bake the cookies,
instead of putting the
dough in the freezer
for 15 minutes, leave it
in the refrigerator,
covered, for at least 1
hour or overnight.
This dough is too
runny at room tem-
perature. It needs to
be cold when you put
it in the oven so that
it doesn't spread too
much.

1 teaspoon baking powder
¼ teaspoon salt
½ cup powdered sugar

Melt the chocolate and butter in a heavy pan over very low heat, stirring occasionally. When the chocolate is almost melted, turn off the
heat and set aside to cool. The heat of the pan will melt the remaining
chocolate.

Put the sugar, eggs and vanilla in a food processor or a large bowl.
Process, or beat with an electric mixer until pale yellow and frothy. Add
the chocolate mixture, and process, or beat on low speed for about 15
seconds, until thoroughly mixed. Add the flour, baking powder and salt,
and pulse for about 10 seconds or beat on low speed just until blended.
Cover the bowl and place it in the freezer for 15 minutes (see Mom
Tip).

Place an oven rack in the middle position and preheat the oven to
350°. Lightly butter the two cookie sheets, or use nonstick sheets.

Spread the powdered sugar on a large plate. Set aside. Remove the
cookie dough from the freezer. Using a teaspoon, shape the dough into
1-inch balls. Roll in the powdered sugar and place them on the cookie
sheets, 3 cookies per row in 4 rows. Bake each batch, one cookie sheet
at a time, for 10 to 12 minutes, or until the top of the cookies are almost
firm. There will be brown and white areas that will look like a bed of
lava.

Remove from the oven and cool on the sheet for about 3 minutes.
Then transfer with a spatula to a cooling rack. Let the cookie sheet cool
for 1 or 2 minutes before reusing so the dough doesn't melt. Store in an
airtight container.

Early 1700s Eager to exploit the popularity of chocolate and to finance their continual wars with each other, Spain, Italy, England and France impose large duties on chocolate imports. Prussia, a country that got lost on its way to the twentieth century, levies two thalers on every chocolate purchase. Demand remains high, so a black market emerges. Smugglers are "rehabilitated" in the state-of-the-art dungeons of the Bastille and the Tower of London.

Spicy Chocolate Cookies

Makes: 48 cookies ⏱ Preparation time: 15 minutes ✋ Chilling time: 15 minutes 🔥 Baking time: 16–20 minutes (8–10 minutes per batch) ⚓ Rating: Easy

Spicy Chocolate Cookies are not overwhelmingly chocolaty, which makes them the perfect dessert after a heavy meal. They're the kind of cookies that you'll loosen your belt one more notch for just to fit a few more in.

2 cups all-purpose flour
½ cup sugar
½ cup unsweetened cocoa powder
½ teaspoon ground cinnamon
½ teaspoon ground cloves
½ teaspoon baking powder
¼ teaspoon baking soda
¼ teaspoon salt

Mom Tip
Honey Albino, whose
recipe this is, likes to
put icing on these
cookies. Any of the
icings in this book will
work well.

¾ cup milk
½ cup corn or canola oil
1 tablespoon whiskey
1 cup (6-ounce package) semisweet chocolate chips
  Butter for greasing (optional)

Put the flour, sugar, cocoa, cinnamon, cloves, baking powder, baking soda and salt in a large bowl and stir to combine. Add the milk, oil and whiskey, and beat with an electric mixer or by hand with a wooden spoon until well blended. Add the chocolate chips and mix thoroughly.

Cover the bowl and place it in the freezer for 15 minutes (or refrigerate the dough for at least 1 hour). Lightly rub two cookie sheets with butter, or use nonstick baking sheets. Set aside.

Place an oven rack in the middle position and preheat the oven to 400°.

Using a teaspoon as a guide, scoop a portion of dough and, with your hands, roll each portion into a 1-inch ball. Place the balls on each cookie sheet, 4 cookies per row in 6 rows. Bake each batch, one cookie sheet at a time, for 8 to 10 minutes. The cookies will be firm to the touch and just beginning to brown.

Remove from the oven and cool on the sheet for about 3 minutes. Then transfer them with a spatula to a cooling rack (see Mom Tip). Store in an airtight container.

Chocolate Shortbread Cookies

Makes: about 50 bite-size cookies ⏱ Preparation time: 15 minutes 🔥 Baking time: 40–50 minutes (20–25 minutes per batch) ☝ Rating: Very Easy

Scotland is the birthplace of shortbread, golf and skirts for men. I doubt I'll ever develop a taste for the latter two (especially golf), but I love shortbread. In fact, it's one of the few nonchocolate desserts that I like. Naturally I wanted to find a way to add chocolate.

> 1 cup (2 sticks) unsalted butter, softened to room
>   temperature
> ⅔ cup powdered sugar
> ⅓ cup unsweetened cocoa powder
> ½ teaspoon vanilla extract
> 1½ cups all-purpose flour
> ¼ teaspoon salt

🐾 Mom Tip
If you like your short-bread thin and crispy, instead of shaping the cookies by hand, divide the dough into 4 pieces. Place 1 section between two sheets of wax paper and roll out the dough ⅛ inch thick. Using cookie cutters, cut dough into shapes. Refrigerate the cut sheet of dough for 12 to 13 minutes to allow the dough to firm up. Carefully pull the wax paper away from each cookie shape and transfer it to an ungreased cookie sheet. Bake for 12 to 13 minutes, or until the cookies are firm to the touch but have not begun to brown. Remove from the oven and cool on the sheet for 5 minutes. Transfer them to a rack to finish cooling. Roll out and bake the other 3 pieces of dough in the same way.

Place an oven rack in the middle position and preheat the oven to 300°. Set out two cookie sheets, but do not grease them.

Put the butter and sugar in a food processor or a large bowl. Process, or beat with an electric mixer until smooth and creamy. Add the cocoa and vanilla, and process or beat until well blended. Add the flour and salt, and pulse for about 10 seconds or beat on low speed just until blended.

Shape the dough into ¾-inch balls (see Mom Tip) and place them on the cookie sheets about 1 inch apart. Leave them round, or flatten them slightly with the heel of your hand. The cookies will not change shape as they bake.

Bake each batch, one sheet at a time, for 20 to 25 minutes, or until the cookies are firm to the touch but have not begun to brown. Remove from the oven and transfer the cookies to a rack to cool. Store in an air-tight container or wrapped in foil or plastic.

Florentines

Makes: 20–30 cookies, depending on size ⏱ Preparation time: 45 minutes 🔥 Baking time: 21–30 minutes (7–10 minutes per batch) ✋ Cooling time: 1 hour (or 15 minutes in refrigerator) ✍ Rating: Not So Easy

I'm always skeptical of sophisticated food. Sophisticated people suck the life out of everything (anyone for a Merchant Ivory film?). So I was leery of Florentines when my mom asked me to try them. Candied fruit and sliced almonds in a chocolate cookie? Never! But after I gave them a try, I realized there's room in this world for both sophisticated European cookies and professional wrestling.

    2 tablespoons unsalted butter + more for greasing
⅓ cup sugar
¼ cup heavy cream
½ cup mixed candied fruit (see Mom Tip 1)

Mom Tip 1
Traditionally, this cookie uses candied orange peel and candied cherries. A good substitute is crystallized ginger, available in gourmet markets. Or you can make Candied Orange Peel (page xx) or simply add an extra ½ cup sliced almonds instead.

Mom Tip 2
Florentines baked on a cookie sheet will be bigger, thinner and less perfectly round than those baked in a muffin pan.

1 cup sliced almonds

2 tablespoons all-purpose flour

6 squares (6 ounces) semisweet chocolate or 1 cup (6-ounce package) semisweet chocolate chips

Place an oven rack in the middle position and preheat the oven to 350°. Lightly rub two cookie sheets or a 12-cup muffin pan with butter, or use nonstick sheets (see Mom Tip 2). Set aside.

Combine the sugar, cream and butter in a small pot and cook over medium heat, stirring occasionally, until the mixture comes to a boil. Cook for 2 minutes over high heat, stirring constantly. Remove from the heat and set aside.

Chop the candied fruit into ¼-inch pieces and add to the milk mixture. Add the almonds and flour, and stir thoroughly.

If you are using cookie sheets, place 8 tablespoons cookie mixture on each sheet, 2 cookies per row in 4 rows. Or place 1 tablespoon cookie mixture in each muffin cup. Bake each batch, one sheet (or muffin pan) at a time, for 7 to 9 minutes. The cookies will spread out and look like a honeycomb, and their outer edges will be brown. The centers will be a lighter brown color, slightly soft and still bubbling. If you are using a muffin pan, bake the cookies for 9 to 10 minutes. (Because they can't spread, they need to bake a little longer.)

When you remove the cookie sheet from the oven, push the edges of the cookies back into a circular shape with a metal or heatproof spatula. (This will not be necessary if you are using a muffin pan.) Cool for about 3 minutes. Loosen the cookies gently with a spatula, or in the case of the muffin pan, with a knife. When the cookies are cool, very carefully transfer them to a cooling rack. Reuse the cookie sheet or muffin pan as necessary. Neither needs to be buttered again.

Melt the chocolate in a heavy frying pan over very low heat, stirring constantly. When the chocolate is almost melted, turn off the heat and set aside to cool. The heat of the pan will melt the remaining chocolate.

Set the cookies on a plate, flat side up. Using a spoon, transfer a teaspoon or more of warm chocolate onto the flat side of each cookie and carefully spread it out to the edges with a knife or rubber spatula. After you have covered all the cookies with chocolate, make wavy lines through the chocolate with the tines of a fork.

Set aside for 1 hour so the chocolate will cool and harden. If you're in a hurry, put the cookies in the refrigerator for 15 minutes. Serve chocolate side up. Store in single layers separated by wax paper, in an airtight container.

Traditional Chocolate Chip Cookies

Makes: 60 cookies ⏱ Preparation time: 15 minutes 🔥 Baking time: 24–32 minutes (6–8 minutes per batch) 🖋 Rating: Easy

This is my "desert island" recipe. If I were stranded in the wild, I wouldn't want hunting and fishing equipment, a radio transmitter or flares. All I'd want would be a mixer, some baking ingredients and, of course, a chocolate-chip tree, and I'd be happy for a couple of decades. I'd bake them in the sun if I had to.

I've made this recipe so many times that I don't even check it for the ingredients anymore, and I'm usually in too big of a rush to bother measuring. So, often the cookies come out tasting different. But that's okay, because the only way to ruin these cookies is to burn them to a crisp. And they're so good, even *that* wouldn't taste too bad.

🦢 Mom Tip
Choosing the right chocolate chips can drive you crazy, especially now that they come in mini, ordinary and mega-chip size, in semisweet, milk chocolate and white chocolate, and in numerous national brands, including Baker's, Ghirardelli, Guittard, Hershey, Nestlé, not to mention the store's own brand. They all taste slightly different, and taste is subjective, so it's a matter of picking the one you like best. We prefer Ghirardelli regular and mega-size chips.

1 cup (2 sticks) unsalted butter, softened to room temperature, + more for greasing
1 cup brown sugar
½ cup sugar
1 large egg
1 teaspoon vanilla extract
2¼ cups all-purpose flour
1 teaspoon baking powder
1 teaspoon baking soda
¼ teaspoon salt
2 cups (12-ounce package) semisweet or milk chocolate chips (see Mom Tip)
1 cup chopped walnuts (optional)

Place an oven rack in the middle position and preheat the oven to 350°. Lightly rub two cookie sheets with butter or use nonstick baking sheets. Set aside.

Put the butter and the sugars in a large bowl. Beat with an electric mixer or a wooden spoon until smooth and creamy. Add the egg and vanilla, and beat again. Add the flour, baking powder, baking soda and salt, and beat on low speed until well blended. Add the chocolate chips and the walnuts, if using, and mix by hand thoroughly.

Using a teaspoon as a guide, scoop a portion of the dough and, with your hands, roll each portion into a 1-inch ball. Place the balls on each cookie sheet, 3 cookies per row in 5 rows. Bake each batch, one cookie sheet at a time, for 6 to 8 minutes. The cookies will be firm to the touch and just beginning to brown. Remove from the oven and cool on the sheet for about 3 minutes. Then transfer them with a spatula to a cooling rack. Let the cookie sheet cool for 1 or 2 minutes more before reusing so the dough doesn't melt. Store in an airtight covered container.

1712 Chocolate is first sold in the American colonies. A Boston apothecary offers chocolate drinks as "restoratives," sort of an eighteenth-century Geritol. The Puritans are skeptical at first, not trusting anything that tastes good, but they soon find that a cup of chocolate is a great way to unwind after a hard day spent burning witches and scrubbing their burlap underpants in the Charles River.

Positively Sinful Chocolate Chip Meringues

Makes: 12 meringues   Preparation time: 30 minutes + 10 minutes for the sauce   Baking time: 20 minutes   Cooling time: 1 hour   Rating: Easy

*S*ometimes less is more—haiku, for example. But most of the time, more is more. You could have just chocolate chip meringues, or just ice cream, or even just chocolate sauce. But this recipe gives you all three. I'll bet that after you eat one of these chocolate chip meringues, you'll want more.

   2 large egg whites
 ¼ teaspoon cream of tartar
 ¼ teaspoon salt
 ¾ cup sugar

⚙ Mom Tip
English Toffee Bits, which are sweet and crunchy, are available near the chocolate chips.

✂! Mom Warning
Meringues cooled in the oven will be dry and crisp and will melt in your mouth. Those cooled on a rack out of the oven will be moist in the middle and will stick in your teeth.

½ teaspoon vanilla extract
1 cup semisweet or milk chocolate chips
1 quart chocolate ice cream
2 cups Bittersweet Dessert Sauce (page 232)
½ cup chopped nuts or English Toffee Bits (see Mom Tip; optional)

Place an oven rack in the middle position and preheat the oven to 300°. Place a 12-inch piece of wax paper on a cookie sheet and set aside.

Put the egg whites in a medium mixing bowl with no traces of grease. Beat with an electric mixer just until the whites are foamy. Add the cream of tartar and salt and continue beating just until the whites form stiff peaks. Do not overbeat. Gently beat in the sugar, 2 tablespoons at a time, until it has been absorbed and the peaks have slightly softened, 1 to 2 minutes. Beat in the vanilla. The mixture will be very thick. Add the chocolate chips, and gently stir them into the meringue with a large spoon.

Roughly divide the mixture into 12 portions, and spoon onto a separate area of the wax paper. Using the back of a spoon, shape each meringue into a 3-inch circle. Bake for about 20 minutes, or until the meringue turns a light golden color. Turn off the oven and cool for 1 hour in the oven with the door closed (see Mom Warning).

When the meringues are finished cooling, remove from the oven. Gently loosen the wax paper from the cookie sheet. If it's stuck, slide a metal or plastic spatula gently under the wax paper to loosen it. Once the wax paper is loose, peel each meringue gently off the paper.

The meringues are very delicate and easily broken, so be careful handling them. If you're not going to use them immediately, store them in a self-sealing plastic bag at room temperature.

To serve, place 1 meringue in a soup bowl. Top with a scoop of the ice cream and pour 2 to 3 tablespoons Bittersweet Dessert Sauce over it. Sprinkle with the chopped nuts or English Toffee Bits, if desired.

Chocolate Chip Peanut Butter Cookies

Makes: 40–45 cookies ⏱ Preparation time: 20 minutes 🔥 Baking time: 30 minutes (10 minutes per batch) ✋ Rating: Easy

Remember the commercial that re-created the invention of Reese's Peanut Butter Cups? A woman is walking down the street eating a chocolate bar, and a man is walking the other way eating a tub of peanut butter. They bump into each other, causing the chocolate and peanut butter to mix. Overcome by the new taste sensation, they immediately check into a motel. (I may be misremembering that last part.) I've never cared for the chocolate–peanut butter combo, so if that idiot had ruined my chocolate bar, I would have pushed him into oncoming traffic. But my mom, who says she's going to have chocolate with peanut butter for her last meal, swears by these cookies. She thinks they're even better than Traditional Chocolate Chip Cookies.

½ cup (1 stick) unsalted butter, softened to room
    temperature, + more for greasing
¾ cup creamy peanut butter
½ cup sugar
½ cup brown sugar
2 large eggs
1 teaspoon vanilla extract
2 cups all-purpose flour
½ teaspoon baking powder
½ teaspoon baking soda
½ teaspoon salt
2 cups (12-ounce package) semisweet chocolate chips
½ cup peanut butter chips
½ cup dry-roasted peanuts

Place an oven rack in the middle position and preheat the oven to 350°. Lightly rub two cookie sheets with butter, or use nonstick baking sheets. Set aside.

Put the butter, peanut butter and the sugars in a large bowl. Beat with an electric mixer or a wooden spoon until smooth and creamy. Add the eggs and vanilla and beat again. Add the flour, baking powder, baking soda and salt, and beat on low speed until well blended. Add the chocolate chips (see Mom Tip), peanut butter chips and peanuts and mix thoroughly.

Using a teaspoon as a guide, scoop a portion of the dough and, with your hands, roll each portion into a ball. Place the balls on each cookie sheet, 3 cookies per row in 5 rows. Flatten the balls with the heel of

If you want a chocolate coating on the top of each cookie, reserve ½ cup chocolate chips when mixing the batter. After the cookies are formed and placed on the cookie sheets, lightly press 5 chocolate chips into the top of each cookie. When the cookies come out of the oven, gently spread those partly melted chocolate chips over the top of each cookie with a knife to make a thin chocolate layer. Cool as directed.

your hand or the tines of a fork so that they spread to about 1½ inches in diameter. Bake each batch, one cookie sheet at a time, for about 10 minutes. The cookies will be firm to the touch and just beginning to brown. Remove from the oven and cool on the sheet for about 3 minutes. Then transfer them with a spatula to a cooling rack. Let the cookie sheet cool for 1 or 2 minutes more before reusing so the dough doesn't melt. Store in an airtight container.

Chocolate-Dipped Biscotti

Makes: 30–40 cookies ⏱ Preparation time: 30 minutes ⚜ Baking time: 40 minutes ✋ Chilling time: 15 minutes ♨ Rating: Not So Easy

B iscotti are usually intended for dipping in coffee, so they tend to have the consistency of petrified wood. But these are too good to be dipped in anything, although I'm sure they would improve the taste of coffee.

Biscotti are not made like other cookies. You don't just dollop out individual spoonfuls and then bake them. In order to get the right shape for biscotti, you have to mold the dough into a long mass, bake it, cut it into slices and bake it again. It makes perfect sense once you try it.

1 cup slivered or sliced almonds
Vegetable oil for greasing
2 cups all-purpose flour
1 cup sugar
⅔ cup unsweetened cocoa powder
1 teaspoon baking soda
¼ teaspoon salt
4 large eggs
1 teaspoon vanilla extract
6 squares (6 ounces) semisweet chocolate

Place an oven rack in the middle position and preheat the oven to 350°.

Spread the almonds on a cookie sheet and bake them for about 5 minutes, or until they begin to turn golden brown. Be careful they don't burn. Remove them from the oven, transfer to a dish and set aside. When the cookie sheet cools off, lightly rub it with vegetable oil. Set aside.

Combine the flour, sugar, cocoa, baking soda and salt in a large bowl. Add the eggs and vanilla, and beat with an electric mixer on low speed for about 15 seconds or with a wooden spoon until well blended. The dough will be very thick and slightly sticky. Stir in the almonds by hand.

Divide the dough in half, and shape each half into a log about 10 inches long and 2 inches wide. Place the logs on the cookie sheet as far apart as possible and flatten them so that they are about 2 inches thick in the center and the surfaces are smooth. Wet your hands to keep the dough from sticking. The dough will spread to a width of about 3 inches. Bake for 20 minutes.

Mom Tip
If you place the
cookies on a metal
rack over the cookie
sheet, you won't have
to turn them, because
the oven heat will
dry both sides of
the cookies at the
same time.

Remove from the oven and cool for 5 minutes. Reduce the oven temperature to 275°.

Using a metal spatula, transfer 1 log to a large cutting board. Using a serrated knife, cut it at a 45° angle into ½-inch slices. Lay each slice, cut side up, on the cookie sheet (see Mom Tip). Repeat with the other log.

Return the cookie sheet to the oven and bake the biscotti for 10 minutes. Turn them over and bake for another 10 minutes. Remove from the oven and cool on a rack.

Melt the chocolate in a heavy frying pan over very low heat, stirring constantly. When the chocolate is almost melted, turn off the heat and set aside to cool. The heat of the pan will melt the remaining chocolate.

Lay a large sheet of wax paper on a tray or cookie sheet. Dip one-third of each cookie into the melted chocolate and set it on the wax paper. Refrigerate the tray of biscotti for 15 minutes so that the chocolate will harden. Store in an airtight container.

Double-Sided Double Chocolate Chip Cookies

Makes: 25–30 double-sided or 50–60 single cookies ⏱ Preparation time: 20 minutes + 10 minutes for the icing 🕯 Baking time: 30 minutes (10 minutes per batch) 🥄 Rating: Easy

When Mom invented these cookies, she started with chocolate chip cookies and asked herself, "Why not make the batter chocolate?" Then, "Why not put icing on them?" And finally, "Why not put two of them together?" When she gets into a chocolate frenzy, Dad has to take away her car keys. She can be dangerous, but we all enjoy eating the results.

Mom Tip
If you're making dou-
ble-sided cookies, flat-
ten each ball of dough
slightly. Otherwise,
the cookies will puff
up, which is fine for
single cookies but will
make round sandwich
cookies.

½ cup (1 stick) unsalted butter, softened to room
      temperature, + more for greasing
½ cup sugar
½ cup brown sugar
1 large egg
1 teaspoon vanilla extract
1 cup all-purpose flour
½ cup unsweetened cocoa powder
½ teaspoon baking soda
½ teaspoon salt
2 cups (12-ounce package) semisweet chocolate chips
1 cup Quick Fudge Icing (page 72)

Place an oven rack in the middle position and preheat the oven to 325°.
Lightly rub two cookie sheets with butter, or use nonstick sheets. Set
aside.

Put the butter and the sugars in a large bowl. Beat with an electric
mixer or a wooden spoon until smooth and creamy. Add the egg and
vanilla, and beat on low speed for about 15 seconds, or about a minute
by hand, until thoroughly mixed. Add the flour, cocoa, baking soda and
salt, and beat just until blended. Add the chocolate chips and mix thoroughly.

Using a teaspoon as a guide, scoop out a portion of dough and, with
your hands, roll each portion into a 1-inch ball. Place the balls on each
cookie sheet, 4 cookies per row in 5 rows (see Mom Tip). Bake each
batch, one cookie sheet at a time, for about 10 minutes. The cookies
will be firm to the touch. Remove from the oven and cool on the sheet

for about 3 minutes. Then transfer them with a spatula to a cooling rack. Let the cookie sheet cool for 1 or 2 minutes more before reusing so the dough doesn't melt.

When the cookies are cool, spread about 1 teaspoon icing on the bottom of one cookie and press the bottom of an equal-size cookie onto the icing, making a double-sided cookie. Continue the process with the remaining cookies. Store in an airtight container.

1789 The English company J. S. Fry and Sons brings chocolate into the Industrial Revolution. Using the newly invented steam engine to grind cacao beans greatly increases production and reduces costs. As a result, English six-year-olds are now able to afford an occasional cup of hot chocolate on their way home from their eighteen-hour shifts at the sweatshop.

Triple Chocolate Brownies

Makes: 25 (1½-inch) squares ⏰ Preparation time: 15 minutes 🔥 Baking time: 20–25 minutes
🏷 Rating: Very Easy

When I order a dessert, I look for the one that has the most chocolate in the title. I feel cheated when I have to settle for just "Chocolate." Triple Chocolate Brownies are right up my alley. With them, you definitely feel that you're getting your money's worth.

2 tablespoons unsalted butter + more for greasing
4 squares (4 ounces) semisweet chocolate
¼ cup water
¼ cup unsweetened cocoa powder
½ cup sugar
2 large eggs
1 teaspoon vanilla extract
½ cup all-purpose flour

🖙 Mom Tip 1
White or semisweet chocolate chips also work well in these brownies.

🖙 Mom Tip 2
If you want a fourth level of chocolate, ice these brownies with Chocolate Butter-cream Icing (page 68), Couldn't-Be-Simpler Chocolate Icing (page 65) or Quick Fudge Icing (page 71).

½ teaspoon baking soda

¼ teaspoon salt

1 cup (6-ounce package) milk chocolate chips
    (see Mom Tip 1)

½ cup chopped walnuts (optional)

Place an oven rack in the middle position and preheat the oven to 350°. Line an 8- or 9-inch square pan with aluminum foil, making sure two ends of the foil overhang the pan by about 2 inches so you can easily lift the brownies out of the pan later. Lightly rub the bottom and sides of the foil with butter. Set aside.

Combine the chocolate, water and butter in a medium, heavy pot over low heat, stirring occasionally. When the chocolate is just melted, turn off the heat and add the cocoa. Stir until combined and set aside to cool for a few minutes.

Add the sugar, eggs and vanilla, and stir until well blended. Add the flour, baking soda and salt, and stir until no flour shows. Stir in the chocolate chips and the walnuts, if using.

Scrape the batter into the pan and bake for 20 to 25 minutes, or until the top feels firm and the brownies pull away from the sides of the pan. Remove from the oven and cool on a rack for 15 minutes. Carefully lift the ends of the foil and remove the brownies from the pan (see Mom Tip 2). Cut into 25 squares and serve. Store in an airtight container or wrapped in foil or plastic wrap.

Movie Star Brownies

Makes: 32 (2-x-1-inch) brownies Preparation time: 15 minutes + 5–10 minutes to make the icing
Baking time: 40 minutes Cooling time: 15 minutes Rating: Easy

 Mom Tip
Donald Russell, the pastry chef at the Four Seasons Hotel in Los Angeles, says the key to this recipe is using Valrhona Guanaja chocolate, available in gourmet stores and by mail order (page 268). However, in a pinch, another semi-sweet or bittersweet chocolate can be substituted.

In her other life, as a journalist who interviews celebrities, my mom frequently attends press events at the Four Seasons Hotel in Los Angeles. After dutifully asking her questions, she then pushes George Clooney or Ashley Judd aside to get at the hotel's signature brownies on the table. Showing a tenacity worthy of Woodward and Bernstein, Mom finally convinced the chef to give her the recipe.

½ cup plus 1 tablespoon unsalted butter + more for greasing
2 squares (2 ounces) bittersweet chocolate (see Mom Tip)
1 square (1 ounce) unsweetened chocolate
2 cups + 2 tablespoons sugar
3 large eggs
¾ teaspoon vanilla extract

1½ cups all-purpose flour
¼ teaspoon salt
¾ cup chopped walnuts
Chocolate Buttercream Icing (page 68)

Place an oven rack in the middle position and preheat the oven to 350°. Line an 8- or 9-inch square pan with aluminum foil, making sure two ends of the foil overhang the pan by about 2 inches so you can easily lift the brownies out of the pan later. Lightly rub the bottom and sides of the foil with butter, and set aside.

Melt both kinds of chocolate and the butter in a heavy frying pan over very low heat, stirring occasionally. When the chocolate is almost melted, turn off the heat and set aside to cool. The heat of the pan will melt the remaining chocolate.

Scrape the cooled chocolate mixture into a large bowl. Add the sugar, and beat with an electric mixer on medium speed or a wooden spoon until smooth. Add the eggs and vanilla, and beat until well incorporated. Add the flour and salt, and beat on low speed just until blended. Add the walnuts and mix thoroughly.

Pour the batter into the pan and bake for about 40 minutes, or until the top feels firm and the sides pull away from the pan. Remove from the oven and cool on a rack for 15 minutes.

When the brownies are cool, carefully lift the ends of the foil and remove from the pan. Spread icing over the top. Cut into 32 bars and serve. Store in an airtight container or wrapped in foil or plastic wrap.

Congo Bars

Makes: 39 (3-x-1-inch) bars ⓧ Preparation time: 15 minutes 🕯 Baking time: 30 minutes 🥄 Rating: Very Easy

These are like chocolate chip cookies, only more so. By adding coconut, white chocolate and walnuts, you're making a good thing better.

½ cup (1 stick) butter, softened to room temperature, + more for greasing
1¾ cups brown sugar
3 large eggs
2 teaspoons vanilla extract
1⅓ cups all-purpose flour
½ cup sweetened shredded coconut
1½ teaspoons baking soda

½ teaspoon salt
1½ cups semisweet mega chocolate chips
½ cup white chocolate chips
½ cup chopped walnuts

Place an oven rack in the middle position and preheat the oven to 350°. Line a 9-x-13-inch baking pan with aluminum foil, making sure two ends of the foil overhang the pan by about 2 inches so you can easily lift the bars out of the pan later. Lightly rub the bottom and sides of the foil with butter, and set aside.

Put the butter and brown sugar in a food processor or a large bowl. Process or beat with an electric mixer or a wooden spoon until smooth and creamy. Add the eggs and vanilla, and process, or beat on low speed for about 15 seconds, or until thoroughly mixed. Add the flour, coconut, baking soda and salt, and pulse for about 10 seconds, or beat on low speed, just until blended. Add both kinds of chocolate chips and the walnuts and mix thoroughly.

Pour the batter into the pan and spread it evenly. Bake for about 30 minutes, or until the top begins to brown and the sides begin to pull away from the pan. Remove from the oven and cool on a rack for 15 minutes. Carefully lift the ends of the foil and remove the bars from the pan. Cut into 39 bars and serve. Store in a closed container or wrapped in foil or plastic wrap.

Early 1800s Napoleon Bonaparte uses chocolate for an energy boost on the battlefield. Two centuries before Randy Newman sings, "Short people have no reason to live," Napoleon proves him wrong by conquering most of Europe. But when his luck—or his chocolate—runs out, he's beaten back by Russian armies.

Intensely Chocolate Cocoa Brownies

Makes: 25 (1½-inch) squares ⏱ Preparation time: 15 minutes 🕯 Baking time: 15–20 minutes
⚓ Rating: Very Easy

W hen regular brownies don't give you the chocolate fix you need, it's time to move on to the harder stuff. Intensely Chocolate Cocoa Brownies are the next best thing to injecting chocolate syrup into your veins.

     ½ cup (1 stick) unsalted butter + more for greasing
     ½ cup unsweetened cocoa powder
     1 cup sugar
     2 large eggs
     1 teaspoon vanilla extract
     ⅔ cup all-purpose flour
     ½ teaspoon baking powder

¼ teaspoon salt

½ cup chopped walnuts (optional)

Place an oven rack in the middle position and preheat the oven to 350°. Line an 8- or 9-inch square pan with aluminum foil, making sure two ends of the foil overhang the pan by about 2 inches so you can easily lift the brownies out of the pan later. Lightly rub the bottom and sides of the foil with butter, and set aside.

Melt the butter in a medium pot over low heat. When it has melted, turn off the heat and stir in the cocoa. Add the sugar, eggs and vanilla, and mix thoroughly.

Add the flour, baking powder and salt and mix just until combined. If you are adding walnuts, stir them in now.

Pour the batter into the foil-lined pan and bake for 15 to 20 minutes, or until the top feels firm. These brownies taste better underbaked rather than overbaked. Remove from the oven and cool on a rack for 15 minutes. Carefully lift the ends of the foil and remove the brownies from the pan. Cut into 25 squares and serve. Store in an airtight container or wrapped in foil or plastic wrap.

Chocolate Oatmeal Brownies

Makes: 48 (1½-inch) squares ⏱ Preparation time: 15 minutes 🔥 Baking time: 25–30 minutes
♨ Rating: Very Easy

By itself, oatmeal is the anti-chocolate. It makes me think of something Oliver Twist would have eaten at the workhouse. But in this recipe, even though it's good for you, it doesn't have that suspiciously healthy taste.

📖 Mom Tip
Quick-cooking oats are usually sold in cylindrical containers in the cereal aisle.

⅔ cup (1 stick + 3 tablespoons) unsalted butter + more for greasing
2 cups (12-ounce package) semisweet chocolate chips
1 cup sugar
2 large eggs
1 teaspoon vanilla extract
1¼ cups all-purpose flour
1 cup quick-cooking oats (see Mom Tip)

1 teaspoon baking powder

¼ teaspoon salt

¾ cup chopped walnuts (optional)

Place an oven rack in the middle position and preheat the oven to 350°. Line a 9-x-13-inch baking pan with aluminum foil, making sure two ends of the foil overhang the pan by about 2 inches so you can easily lift the brownies out of the pan later. Lightly rub the bottom and sides of the foil with butter, and set aside.

Melt the butter and 1 cup of the chocolate chips in a small, heavy pot over very low heat, stirring occasionally. When the chocolate is almost melted, turn off the heat and set aside to cool. The heat of the pot will melt the remaining chocolate.

Put the sugar, eggs and vanilla in a large bowl. Beat with an electric mixer on high speed for about 2 minutes, or much longer by hand, until pale yellow and frothy. Add the chocolate mixture and beat on low speed for about 15 seconds, or about a minute by hand, until thoroughly mixed. Add the flour, oats, baking powder and salt and mix just until blended. Add the remaining cup of chocolate chips and the walnuts, if using, and mix thoroughly.

Pour the batter into the pan and spread it evenly. It will be very thick. Bake for 25 to 30 minutes, or until a cake tester or knife inserted into the center comes out clean. Remove from the oven and cool on a rack for 15 minutes. Carefully lift the ends of the foil and remove the brownies from the pan. Cut into 48 squares and serve. Store in a closed container or wrapped in foil or plastic wrap.

Peanut Butter Chocolate Brownies

Makes: 25 (1½-inch) squares ⏲ Preparation time: 15 minutes ⚜ Baking time: 30 minutes
⚖ Rating: Very Easy

My parents went to college in the 1960s, a time when brownies frequently included illicit ingredients. My wholesome mother preferred to lace her brownies with peanut butter, which she'd eat while grooving to the latest concept album by the Monkees. It was a great time to be alive.

2 squares (2 ounces) unsweetened chocolate
¼ cup (½ stick) unsalted butter, softened to room
        temperature, + more for greasing
¼ cup chunky peanut butter
1 cup dark brown sugar
2 large eggs
1 teaspoon vanilla extract

🖙 Mom Tip
For a more chocolaty brownie, add 1 cup semisweet chocolate chips when you add the peanuts.

½ cup all-purpose flour

½ teaspoon baking powder

¼ teaspoon salt

¼ cup chopped dry roasted peanuts (see Mom Tip)

Place an oven rack in the middle position and preheat the oven to 350°. Line an 8- or 9-inch square pan with aluminum foil, making sure the ends of the foil overhang the pan by about 2 inches so you can easily lift the brownies out of the pan later. Lightly rub the bottom and sides of the foil with butter and set aside.

Melt the chocolate in a small, heavy pot over very low heat, stirring constantly. When the chocolate is almost melted, turn off the heat and set aside to cool. The heat of the pot will melt the remaining chocolate.

Put the butter, peanut butter and brown sugar in a large bowl. Beat with an electric mixer on high speed or a wooden spoon until smooth and creamy. Add the eggs, vanilla and melted chocolate and beat until well incorporated. Add the flour, baking powder and salt and mix just until blended. Add the peanuts and mix thoroughly.

Pour the batter into the pan and bake for about 30 minutes, or until the top feels firm and the sides pull away from the pan. Remove from the oven and cool on a rack for 15 minutes. Carefully lift the ends of the foil and remove the brownies from the pan. Cut into 25 squares and serve. Store in an airtight container or wrapped in foil or plastic wrap.

Brownie Macaroons

Makes: 48 (1½-inch) squares Preparation time: 15 minutes Baking time: 20–25 minutes
Rating: Very Easy

When I was growing up, my dad would occasionally come home with a coconut and have me and my sister Bonnie try to open it. We would pound on it, jump on it, throw it against the wall of the garage, but we could never crack it. Eventually, Dad would take a hammer and put it out of its misery. Luckily, coconut growers now do all that hard work for you.

10 tablespoons (1 stick plus 2 tablespoons) unsalted butter, softened to room temperature, + more for greasing
3 squares (3 ounces) unsweetened chocolate
2 squares (2 ounces) semisweet chocolate
¾ cup brown sugar
½ cup sugar

※☀! Mom Warning
If you overbake these macaroons, they will be dry, so remove them from the oven as soon as the top feels firm to the touch.

2 large eggs
2 teaspoons vanilla extract
1 cup all-purpose flour
1 teaspoon baking powder
¼ teaspoon salt
1 cup sweetened shredded coconut

Place an oven rack in the middle position and preheat the oven to 350°.

Line a 9-x-13-inch baking pan with aluminum foil, making sure two ends of the foil overhang the pan by about 2 inches so you can easily lift the brownies out of the pan later. Lightly rub the bottom and sides of the foil with butter, and set aside.

Melt both kinds of chocolate in a small, heavy pot over very low heat, stirring constantly. When the chocolate is almost melted, turn off the heat and set aside to cool. The heat of the pot will melt the remaining chocolate.

Put the butter and the sugars in a large bowl. Beat with an electric mixer on high speed or a wooden spoon until smooth and creamy. Add the eggs, vanilla and cooled chocolate, and beat until well incorporated. Add the flour, baking powder and salt, and beat on low speed just until blended. Add the coconut and mix thoroughly.

Pour the batter into the pan and spread it evenly. It will be very thick. Bake for 20 to 25 minutes, or until a cake tester or knife inserted into the center comes out clean (see Mom Warning). Remove from the oven and cool on a rack for 15 minutes. Carefully lift the ends of the foil and remove the macaroons from the pan. Cut into 48 squares and serve. Store in an airtight container or wrapped in foil or plastic wrap.

☼ Mid 1800s With solid chocolate in higher demand, chocolate drinks are no longer fashion-
able. Ever eager for the latest upgrade, the aristocracy abandons hot chocolate to the Oliver
Twists of the world. Economists call this the "Chocolate Trickle-Down Theory."

Chocolate-Lovers' Lemon Squares

Makes: 25 (1½-inch) squares ⏱ Preparation time: 25 minutes 🔥 Baking time: 33–40 minutes
🖐 Chilling time: 1 hour ✌ Rating: Easy

These aren't your grandmother's community bake sale lemon squares. These are lemon squares that you will want to keep for yourself, or at least charge more than a quarter for. They have a thick chocolate cookie crust.

CRUST

    ½ cup (1 stick) unsalted butter, softened to room
          temperature, + more for greasing

    ⅓ cup powdered sugar

    ¼ cup unsweetened cocoa powder

    ¾ cup all-purpose flour

    ¼ teaspoon salt

    1 teaspoon vanilla extract

Mom Tip
If you're in a hurry, use bottled lemon juice, often available in the bottled fruit juice section, and bottled grated lemon peel, available in the spice section at the grocery store.

FILLING

1 lemon (see Mom Tip)
1 cup sugar
2 large eggs
2 tablespoons all-purpose flour
½ teaspoon baking powder
¼ cup powdered sugar (optional)

TO MAKE THE CRUST: Place an oven rack in the middle position and preheat the oven to 350°. Line an 8- or 9-inch square pan with aluminum foil, making sure two ends of the foil overhang the pan by about 2 inches so you can easily lift the squares out of the pan later. Lightly rub the bottom and sides of the foil with butter and set aside.

Combine the butter and powdered sugar in a food processor or a large bowl. Process for about 1 minute, or beat with an electric mixer until smooth, creamy and dark brown. Add the cocoa, flour, salt and vanilla and pulse or beat on low speed just until blended.

Press the dough into an even layer in the foil-lined pan. Bake for 15 to 20 minutes, or until the crust feels firm to the touch but has not begun to brown. Remove from the oven and cool on a rack.

TO MAKE THE FILLING: Grate the lemon rind against the smallest holes of a grater until the entire yellow surface has been grated off and the white pith shows (but don't grate the pith—it's bitter). You will have about 2 teaspoons grated peel. Cut the lemon in half and squeeze out the juice. You will have about 3 tablespoons juice.

Combine the sugar, eggs, grated lemon rind, lemon juice, flour and baking powder in a medium bowl and stir well until combined. Pour over the baked crust, making sure it completely covers the crust. Bake for 18 to 20 minutes, or until the filling has begun to brown.

Remove from the oven and cool on a rack for 15 minutes. Refrigerate, covered, until needed. Carefully lift the ends of the foil and remove the lemon squares from the pan. Cut into 25 squares. Sprinkle with powdered sugar, if you like (see Mom Tip, page 40). Serve cold. Store in the refrigerator in an airtight container or wrapped in foil or plastic.

Chocolate Turtle Bars

Serves: 16–20 🕐 Preparation time: 40 minutes 🔥 Baking time: 15–20 minutes ✋ Chilling time: 4 hours 👆 Rating: Not So Easy

When we celebrated my grandmother's eighty-second birthday this year, we took her to a restaurant. The highlight was dessert: this caramel-flavored chocolate-nut bar. I felt genuinely guilty beating Grandma to the last piece.

The pastry chef of the restaurant, Chez Melange in Redondo Beach, California, was kind enough to give us the recipe. When we made it at home, I should have sent Grandma a piece to make amends. She's been sharpening her elbows so she won't lose out next year.

CRUST

¼ cup (½ stick) unsalted butter, softened to room
   temperature, + more for greasing

¼ cup brown sugar

¼ teaspoon salt

1½ cups chopped pecans

TOPPING

8 squares (8 ounces) bittersweet chocolate

1 cup heavy cream

¼ cup (½ stick) unsalted butter

1 tablespoon corn syrup

1 tablespoon unsweetened cocoa powder

CHOCOLATE CARAMEL SAUCE

½ cup sugar

⅓ cup heavy cream

2 tablespoons unsalted butter

¼ cup semisweet chocolate chips

1 teaspoon vanilla extract

   Dash salt

Place an oven rack in the middle position and preheat the oven to 325°.
Line an 8- or 9-inch square pan with aluminum foil, making sure two
ends of the foil overhang the pan by about 2 inches so you can easily
lift the bars out of the pan later. Lightly rub the bottom and sides of the
foil with butter and set aside.

☼! Mom Warning
If you cover this dessert before it has cooled, water may condense and drip onto the surface of the chocolate.

☞ Mom Tip
Before cutting the bars, Chez Melange pastry chef Maureen Clune recommends dipping the knife into hot water and reheating as necessary, so that it will cut smoothly.

TO MAKE THE CRUST: Put the brown sugar, butter and salt in a food processor or a large bowl. Process, or beat with an electric mixer just until blended. Add the pecans, and process or beat just until mixed.

Press the dough into an even layer in the foil-lined pan. Bake for 15 to 20 minutes, or until the dough feels firm to the touch and has begun to brown. Remove from the oven and set on a rack to cool.

MEANWHILE, MAKE THE TOPPING: Combine all the ingredients in a medium, heavy pot and place over low heat. Stir continuously until the chocolate has melted and the mixture is smooth. The cocoa tends to clump, so stir thoroughly. Remove from the heat and cool for 5 minutes.

Pour the warm chocolate filling over the cooled crust. When the filling has cooled, refrigerate, covered, for at least 4 hours (see Mom Warning).

TO MAKE THE CHOCOLATE CARAMEL SAUCE: Combine the sugar and cream in a small, heavy pot and stir to dissolve the sugar. Place over medium-high heat, stirring occasionally. When the mixture comes to a boil, let it cook for 2 or 3 minutes, or until it begins to darken.

Remove from the heat and stir in the butter and chocolate chips. When they have melted, add the vanilla and salt, and stir until thoroughly combined. Use warm or at room temperature.

When you are ready to serve the bars, carefully lift the ends of the foil and remove the bars from the pan. Cut into 1-x-2-inch bars (see Mom Tip). Put 2 bars on each plate and top with a spoonful of the sauce. For extra decoration, drizzle another spoonful of sauce on the plate. Cover and refrigerate leftovers. Store any extra sauce in a closed container in the refrigerator.

Jaffa Squares

Makes: 25 (1½-inch) squares   Preparation time: 15 minutes   Baking time: 30–35 minutes
Rating: Easy

E ver heard of a Jaffa cake? Unless you've been to England, probably not. They're little cookies covered with chocolate and filled with what the package calls a "smashing orangey bit." They taste really good, but for some reason they're available in this country only on the black market. Never fear, said my mom. She went into her lab, and after some strange noises and a few puffs of smoke, emerged with Jaffa Squares. I think they're smashing.

½ cup (1 stick) unsalted butter, softened to room
    temperature, + more for greasing
½ cup sugar
1¼ cups all-purpose flour
⅔ cup apricot jam
1 cup (6-ounce package) semisweet chocolate chips

Place an oven rack in the middle position and preheat the oven to 350°.
Line an 8- or 9-inch square pan with aluminum foil, making sure two
ends of the foil overhang the pan by about 2 inches so you can easily
lift the squares out of the pan later. Lightly rub the bottom and sides of
the foil with butter and set aside.

Put the butter and sugar in a food processor or a large bowl. Process,
or beat with an electric mixer on high speed until smooth and creamy.
Add the flour, and pulse for about 10 seconds, or beat on low speed until
blended. Press the dough into the foil-lined pan and bake for 25 to 30
minutes, or until the top is firm and the cake is just beginning to brown.

Remove from the oven and spread the jam evenly over the top. Sprinkle the chocolate chips over the jam. Bake for another 5 minutes, or
until the chips have begun to melt. Remove from the oven and, with a
wide-bladed knife, spread the melting chocolate over the jam so that it
becomes an icing. Cool on a rack for 15 minutes. Carefully lift the ends
of the foil and remove the bars from the pan. Cut into 25 squares (see
Mom Tip) and serve. Store in the refrigerator in an airtight container or
wrapped in foil or plastic wrap.

1875 In Switzerland, Daniel Peter invents milk chocolate, which has dominated the chocolate market ever since. But, as every action has an equal and opposite reaction, this development also produces the chocolate snob, an ornery sort who prefers his chocolate dark, bitter and expensive.

Blondies Topped with Chocolate and Nuts

Makes: 25 (1½-inch) squares 🕐 Preparation time: 15 minutes 🔥 Baking time: 22 minutes
✋ Cooling time: 15 minutes ✍ Rating: Easy

~~~~~~

*B*londies are a little like chocolate chip cookies without the chocolate chips but with a milk chocolate icing. My mom once made a batch for me to pass around on a group ski trip. After I tried them, I refused to share them with the rest of the people on the bus. Chocolate turns me into a miser.

    ½ cup (1 stick) unsalted butter + more for greasing
    1 cup brown sugar
    2 large eggs
    1 teaspoon vanilla extract
    1 cup all-purpose flour
    ¼ teaspoon salt
    ¼ teaspoon baking powder

🍳 Mom Tip 1
Milk chocolate baking bars are available near the chocolate chips. If you can't find any, use ⅔ cup milk chocolate chips instead.

🍳 Mom Tip 2
If you line the baking pan with foil, you'll be able to remove the blondies in one piece and cut them neatly on a cutting board. Because of their topping, they are messy to get out of the pan otherwise.

⅛ teaspoon baking soda
1 4-ounce milk chocolate baking bar (see Mom Tip 1)
½ cup chopped walnuts

Melt the butter in a medium pot over low heat. When it has melted, turn off the heat and add the brown sugar. Stir until thoroughly combined and cool for about 10 minutes.

Place an oven rack in the middle position and preheat the oven to 350°. Line an 8- or 9-inch square pan with aluminum foil, making sure two ends of the foil overhang the pan by about 2 inches (see Mom Tip 2). Lightly rub the bottom and sides of the foil with butter, and set aside.

When the butter mixture has cooled, add the eggs and vanilla, and mix thoroughly. Add the flour, salt, baking powder and baking soda and mix just until combined.

Pour the batter into the foil-lined pan and bake for about 20 minutes, or until the top has begun to brown and feels firm. Break the chocolate baking bar into large pieces. Remove the blondies from the oven, lay the chocolate pieces on top and return to the oven for 2 minutes to allow the chocolate to begin to melt.

Remove from the oven and, using a knife, spread the melted chocolate as evenly as possible over the top of the cake. Sprinkle the nuts on top and gently press them into the chocolate. Cool on a rack for about 15 minutes, or until the chocolate topping has begun to firm up. Carefully lift the ends of the foil and remove the blondies from the pan. Cut into 25 squares and serve. Store in an airtight container or wrapped in foil.

1879 Rodolphe Lindt invents "conching," a process to make chocolate smoother. The slogan for the new creation, dubbed "fondant," could have been "Try our new chocolate — now with fewer lumps!" It would have sounded better in French.

Chocolate Crispy Rice Treats

Makes: 25 (1½-inch) squares   Preparation time: 10 minutes   Baking time: None
Chilling time: 15 minutes or 1 hour   Rating: Very Easy

I first discovered this crispy delicacy at summer camp. They were served every evening at the campfire and were a great antidote to the hippie sing-alongs that we had to sit through. I now enjoy them at home (the chocolate version, of course), without being bothered by mosquitoes or having to chant a nonsensical ditty about "a horse with no name."

Mom Tip
Chunky peanut butter will provide pieces of peanut in these treats, and smooth peanut butter will make them taste less peanuty.

1½ cups semisweet chocolate chips
½ cup peanut butter (see Mom Tip)
4 cups crispy rice cereal

Line an 8- or 9-inch square pan with aluminum foil, making sure two ends of the foil overhang the pan by about 2 inches so you can easily lift the treats from the pan later. Lightly rub the bottom and sides of the foil with butter and set aside.

Combine the chocolate chips and peanut butter in a medium, heavy pot and place over low heat. Stir continuously. When the chocolate is almost melted, turn off the heat and set aside to cool. The heat of the pot will melt the remaining chocolate.

Stir in the crispy cereal and mix until it is completely coated with the chocolate–peanut butter mixture.

Scrape the mixture into the pan and freeze for 15 minutes or refrigerate for 1 hour, or until the top feels cool and firm. Carefully lift the ends of the foil and remove the treats from the pan. Cut into 25 squares and serve. Store in the refrigerator in an airtight container or wrapped in foil or plastic wrap.

No-Bake Chocolate Granola Bars

Makes: 16 (4-x-1-inch) bars ⏱ Preparation time: 15 minutes 🔥 Baking time: None ✋ Chilling time: 15 minutes or 1 hour ✍ Rating: Very Easy

~~~~~~

*E*verybody's mother sends them to school with granola bars. After lunch period, you see piles of uneaten granola bars in the trash. These chocolate granola bars won't suffer the same fate.

½ cup (1 stick) unsalted butter + more for greasing
⅓ cup brown sugar
¼ cup unsweetened cocoa powder
1¾ cups granola
½ cup semisweet chocolate chips
¼ cup chopped walnuts
1 teaspoon vanilla extract

☀! Mom Warning
It's easier to cut these
bars when they are
cold; they may crum-
ble when warm. Use
bits of the crumble as
a topping for ice
cream.

Line an 8- or 9-inch square pan with aluminum foil, making sure two ends of the foil overhang the pan by about 2 inches so you can easily lift the bars out of the pan later. Lightly rub the bottom and sides of the foil with butter, and set aside.

Combine the butter, brown sugar and cocoa in a medium, heavy pot over medium heat, stirring occasionally, for about 3 minutes, or until the butter has melted. Remove from the heat and stir in the granola, chocolate chips, walnuts and vanilla.

Scrape the batter into the pan, and freeze for 15 minutes or refrigerate for 1 hour, or until the top feels cool and firm. Carefully lift the ends of the foil and remove the granola bars from the pan. Cut into 16 bars and serve (see Mom Warning). Store in the refrigerator in a closed container or wrapped in foil.

Pies/
Pie Crusts

P ies are usually *thought* of as an elaborate way *to* get fruit into your system. I've been so brainwashed by apple pie, cherry pie, blueberry pie and *the rest of them that the* concept of chocolate pie seems a little strange. I say, Watch out apple pie. If I have my way, someday they'll be saying, "As American as chocolate mousse pie."

Brownie Fudge Pie ★ 138

Chocolate Mousse Pie ★ 140

Chocolate Pecan Pie ★ 142

Chocolate Meringue Pie ★ 144

Chocolate Angel Pie ★ 147

Miniature Chocolate Turnovers ★ 150

Can't-Fail Pie Crust ★ 152

Chocolate Crumb Crust ★ 155

Peanutty Pie Crust ★ 157

Cookie Dough Pie Crust ★ 160

Easy Cocoa Crust ★ 163

Brownie Fudge Pie

Serves: 8–10 Preparation time: 20 minutes + 10–80 minutes to make the pie crust Baking time: 25 minutes Cooling time: 1 hour (to serve at room temperature); 3 hours (to serve cold) Rating: Easy

I think Brownie Fudge Pie tastes best cold. But who can wait? I've found that each piece I eat gets gradually better as the pie cools, and by the time it's just right, I've finished the entire pie.

8 squares (8 ounces) bittersweet chocolate
¼ cup (½ stick) unsalted butter
¾ cup brown sugar
3 large eggs
1 tablespoon instant coffee granules
2 teaspoons vanilla extract
½ teaspoon salt
¼ cup all-purpose flour

Mom Tip 1
You can change the
taste of this pie by
varying the crust: try
Can't Fail Pie Crust
(page 152), Cookie
Dough Pie Crust
(page 160) or
Peanutty Pie Crust
(page 157).

Mom Tip 2
Refrigerated, rolled-
out, ready-to-bake pie
crusts are usually
available near the
tubed biscuits at the
grocery store; Pills-
bury is a good brand.
Graham cracker
crusts are also avail-
able, usually in the
baking section.

½ cup chopped walnuts, + 12 walnut halves
1 unbaked pie crust (see Mom Tips 1 and 2)

Place an oven rack in the middle position and preheat the oven to 375°.

Melt the chocolate and butter in a heavy frying pan over very low heat, stirring occasionally. When the chocolate is almost melted, turn off the heat and set aside to cool. The heat of the pan will melt the remaining chocolate.

Beat the brown sugar and eggs together in a mixing bowl with an electric mixer for about 2 minutes on high speed or about 5 minutes with a wooden spoon until pale yellow and frothy. Add the chocolate mixture, and beat at low speed or by hand for about 15 seconds, or until thoroughly mixed. Add the coffee granules, vanilla and salt, and beat at low speed for about 15 seconds, or by hand until thoroughly mixed.

Stir the flour and chopped walnuts together in a small bowl. Transfer to the chocolate mixture and beat at low speed or by hand for a few seconds, or until just mixed.

Pour the filling into the unbaked pie crust. Gently place the walnut halves in a circular pattern on the top of the pie. Bake for about 25 minutes, or until the top has formed a firm crust. The filling will be more like fudge than cake. Remove from the oven and cool on a rack from 1 to 3 hours. Serve at room temperature or cold. Cover and refrigerate leftovers.

Chocolate Mousse Pie

Serves: 10–12 ⏱ Preparation time: 15 minutes + 20–110 minutes to make the crust 🔥 Baking time: None ✋ Cooling time: 30 minutes ✍ Rating: Easy

This is probably the richest recipe in the book. Make sure you're not going to need to use your brain for a few hours after eating it. All functions except "drool" will be turned off.

☀! Mom Warning
This dessert contains raw eggs.

12 squares (12 ounces) semisweet chocolate
2 large eggs + 4 large yolks (see Mom Warning)
1 teaspoon vanilla extract (see Mom Tip)
1 baked pie crust (see Mom Tip 1, page 139)

Place an oven rack in the middle position and preheat the oven to 350°.

Melt the chocolate in a heavy frying pan over very low heat, stirring constantly. When the chocolate is almost melted, turn off the heat and set aside to cool. The heat of the pan will melt the remaining chocolate.

Mom Tip
To change the flavor of the chocolate, substitute 1 teaspoon Kahlúa, Cointreau or another fruit-flavored liqueur for the vanilla.

Put the eggs, egg yolks and vanilla in a large bowl and beat with an electric mixer or a wooden spoon until smooth. Stir in the cooled melted chocolate and mix until the chocolate is fully incorporated.

Pour the filling into the baked pie crust and smooth the top with the back of a spoon. Cool for about 30 minutes and serve. This pie tastes best when it is served warm. Cover and refrigerate leftovers. When cold, the pie will taste more like fudge than mousse.

Chocolate Pecan Pie

Serves: 8–10 ⏱ Preparation time: 20 minutes + 10–80 minutes to make the crust 🔥 Baking time: 45–50 minutes ✋ Cooling time: 1 hour (to serve at room temperature); 3 hours (to serve cold) ✊ Rating: Easy

~~~~~~

My brother-in-law Dan ordered a slice of pecan pie at a diner. He asked for it à la mode, but with chocolate ice cream instead of vanilla. The owner refused to give it to him. She said chocolate would ruin the pie. Dan indignantly skipped dessert.

To chocolate purists, everything tastes better with chocolate. In this recipe, the chocolate's on the inside, out of the reach of meddlers.

Mom Tip 1
Use maple syrup if you don't have light corn syrup.

2 squares (2 ounces) semisweet chocolate
2 tablespoons unsalted butter
1 cup light corn syrup (see Mom Tip 1)
⅓ cup sugar
3 large eggs

Mom Tip 2
If you can't find pecan halves, use walnut halves; they taste similar.

1 teaspoon vanilla extract

¼ teaspoon salt

1 cup chopped pecans + 1 cup pecan halves (see Mom Tip 2)

1 tablespoon all-purpose flour

¼ cup brewed coffee, or 1 tablespoon instant coffee granules dissolved in ¼ cup hot water

1 unbaked pie crust (see Mom Tip 1, page 139)

Place an oven rack in the middle position and preheat the oven to 400°.

Melt the chocolate and butter in a heavy frying pan over very low heat, stirring occasionally. When the chocolate is almost melted, turn off the heat and set aside to cool. The heat of the pan will melt the remaining chocolate.

Combine the corn syrup, sugar, eggs, vanilla and salt in a large bowl and mix thoroughly. The mixture will look lumpy. Combine the 1 cup chopped pecans and the flour in a small bowl, and stir so that the nuts are covered with flour. Add the nuts to the egg mixture and stir thoroughly. Add the chocolate mixture and the coffee and mix well.

Pour the filling into the pie crust. Place the pecan halves in circles over the filling.

Bake for 15 minutes. Turn down the temperature to 350° and bake for another 30 to 35 minutes, or until the pie begins to brown. Remove from the oven and cool on a rack, 1 to 3 hours. Don't worry if the top develops cracks as the pie cools. Serve at room temperature or cold. Cover and refrigerate leftovers.

Chocolate Meringue Pie

Serves: 8–10 ⏱ Preparation time: 35 minutes + 20–110 minutes to make the crust 🔥 Baking time: 7–8 minutes ✋ Cooling time: 1 hour 🥄 Rating: Not So Easy

~~~~~~

No doubt you've been lured, as I have, by a slice of chocolate meringue pie in a pastry case. It looks like pure chocolate, but after a few bites, you realize that the filling tastes as though it came out of an aerosol can. This Chocolate Meringue Pie delivers on the promise.

4 squares (4 ounces) unsweetened chocolate
4 large eggs
2½ cups milk
⅔ cup sugar + ½ cup sugar
¼ cup cornstarch
½ teaspoon salt
2 tablespoons unsalted butter

2   teaspoons vanilla extract
½   teaspoon cream of tartar
1   baked pie crust (see Mom Tip 1, page 139)

Place an oven rack in the middle position and preheat the oven to 425°.

Melt the chocolate in a small, heavy pot over very low heat, stirring constantly. When the chocolate is almost melted, turn off the heat and set aside to cool. The heat of the pot will melt the remaining chocolate.

Separate the eggs, putting the yolks in a medium, heavy pot and the whites in a large glass or metal bowl with no traces of grease. Set the whites aside.

Beat the egg yolks for a few seconds with a fork, and stir in the milk. Add the ⅔ cup sugar, cornstarch and salt and mix until combined. Place over medium heat, stirring constantly. Cook for about 5 minutes, or until bubbles form around the edges and the mixture begins to thicken. Add the melted chocolate, butter and vanilla, and stir to incorporate. Remove from the heat and set aside while making the meringue.

Using an electric mixer, beat the egg whites until they are foamy. Add the cream of tartar, and continue beating just until stiff peaks form. Do not overbeat. Gently beat in the remaining ½ cup sugar, 2 tablespoons at a time, until all the sugar has been absorbed and the peaks have slightly softened, 1 to 2 minutes.

Immediately transfer the filling to the baked pie shell. Gently spoon the meringue on top and spread it with the back of a spoon so that it completely covers the filling and touches the edge of the pie crust (see Mom Warning). Swirl the meringue with the back of the spoon to make little peaks.

Bake for 7 to 8 minutes, or until the peaks begin to brown. The meringue is done when it's partly golden brown, partly white. Check after 5 minutes and then every minute thereafter to make sure it doesn't burn. Remove from the oven and cool on a rack for 1 hour. Serve at room temperature or cold. Cover and refrigerate leftovers.

Chocolate Angel Pie

Serves: 8 Preparation time: 30 minutes Baking time: 1 hour Cooling time: 1 hour Chilling time: 1 hour Rating: Not So Easy

C hocolate Angel Pie has a meringue crust, and the chocolate filling is so light that if it weren't attached to the crust it would fly up and get caught in the ceiling fan. It was a popular dessert during the first half of the twentieth century, and the recipe was handed down to my mom's friend Julie Riskin, and then across to us. To me, it tastes best refrigerated, which must have been a problem way back when, since refrigeration hadn't been invented yet. Maybe Julie's mother-in-law and grandmother-in-law had to wait for the iceman to come around before they cooked it. Luckily, it also tastes good warm.

⟡ Mom Tip 1
Baker's German's
Chocolate comes in
4-ounce boxes. It is
sweeter than other
baking chocolate. For
a less sweet taste,
substitute 4 squares
(4 ounces) bitter-
sweet or semisweet
chocolate.

4 large egg whites

½ teaspoon cream of tartar

1 cup sugar

4 ounces (1 box) Baker's German's Sweet Chocolate
(see Mom Tip 1)

3 tablespoons brewed coffee or 1 teaspoon instant coffee
granules dissolved in 3 tablespoons hot water

1 tablespoon cognac or brandy or 1 teaspoon vanilla extract

1 cup heavy cream

1 square (1 ounce) semisweet chocolate, finely chopped
(optional, for decorating)

Place an oven rack in the middle position and preheat the oven to 275°. Wipe a 9-inch pie pan with vegetable oil and set aside.

Put the egg whites into a large metal or ceramic bowl with no traces of grease, and beat with an electric mixer until foamy. Add the cream of tartar, and continue beating just until they form stiff peaks. Do not over-beat. Gently beat in the sugar, 2 tablespoons at a time, until all the sugar has been absorbed and the peaks have slightly softened, 1 to 2 minutes.

Scrape the meringue into the pie pan and spread it over the bottom and up the sides. Try to make the sides higher than the middle. Bake for about 1 hour, or until the meringue turns a light golden color. Turn off the oven and cool for 1 hour in the oven with the door closed.

While the pie crust is cooling, melt the sweet chocolate in a small, heavy pot over very low heat, stirring constantly. When the chocolate is almost melted, turn off the heat and set aside to cool. The heat of the pan will melt the remaining chocolate.

⟡ **Mom Tip 2**
To make chocolate flakes, either cut the chocolate finely with a sharp knife or use a vegetable peeler to scrape off thin slices of chocolate over the top of the pie.

Stir in the coffee and the liquor or vanilla. Stir until well incorporated and set aside.

Pour the cream into a medium bowl, and beat with an electric mixer until it thickens, 1 to 2 minutes (see Mom Tip, page 171).

Pour the chocolate mixture over the cream and mix them gently with a rubber spatula, scooping up the cream from the bottom of the bowl and turning the spatula over repeatedly until no white is showing. Pour the filling into the center of the cooled meringue and spread it to within an inch of the rim. Decorate with the finely chopped chocolate, if you like (see Mom Tip 2).

Refrigerate, uncovered, for 1 hour. If you plan to refrigerate the pie any longer before serving, cover it with plastic wrap or aluminum foil. Serve cold. Cover and refrigerate leftovers.

1900 Milton Hershey begins selling the nickel Hershey Bar. Made from a secret combination of ingredients and the milk of local cows, the Hershey Bar makes America fall in love with chocolate. Hershey uses the same formula today, though hopefully not the same cows.

Miniature Chocolate Turnovers

Makes: 12 bite-size turnovers Preparation time: 10 minutes Thawing time: 30 minutes
 Baking time: 15 minutes Rating: Very Easy

Every evening after dinner when we were growing up, my sister and I would scour the cupboards and the freezer for chocolate desserts. If we found none, Mom would offer apple turnovers from a package she kept in the freezer. We would sigh and reluctantly settle for them. An apple turnover to a chocoholic is like chewing gum to a heavy smoker: a poor substitute. But with *these* turnovers, there are no sighs until *after* you finish them.

 Mom Tip 1
Puff pastry sheets come two to a box and are available in the frozen food section of most supermarkets.

 Mom Tip 2
Any type of semisweet chocolate can be used, including baking squares, baking bars or candy bars.

1 tablespoon all-purpose flour
1 sheet (half of 17¼-ounce package) frozen puff pastry (see Mom Tip 1)
3 squares (3 ounces) semisweet chocolate (see Mom Tip 2) or ½ cup semisweet chocolate chips

Sprinkle the flour onto a large cutting board or piece of wax paper. Remove the sheet of puff pastry from the package and place on the floured cutting board or wax paper to thaw for 30 minutes.

Place an oven rack in the middle position and preheat the oven to 400°. Set out the cookie sheet, but do not grease it.

While waiting for the puff pastry to thaw, chop the chocolate into 12 roughly equal portions (if using squares of chocolate). Set aside.

When the puff pastry is pliable, gently unfold it. Then, using a rolling pin, flatten it slightly into a 12-x-9-inch rectangle. With a knife, cut the pastry into 3-inch squares. Transfer the squares to the cookie sheet and place a portion of the chocolate in the center of each square. Fold each square into a triangle, moisten the inside edges with water and firmly press the edges together.

Bake for 15 minutes, or until the turnovers have puffed and are golden brown. Remove from the oven and serve immediately or within 15 minutes, so that the chocolate will still be warm. Otherwise, reheat for 5 minutes in a 350° oven before serving. Store in an airtight container.

Can't-Fail Pie Crust

Makes: 1 pie crust ⏱ Preparation time: 10 minutes 🔥 Baking time: 8–12 minutes ♨ Rating: Easy

C an't-Fail" makes me think of that universal prelude to getting lost, the words "You can't miss it." Of course you can fail making this crust, but we're trying to start you out with a positive attitude. It really is pretty easy, though.

   1 cup all-purpose flour + more for rolling
½ teaspoon salt
¼ cup canola oil or corn oil
¼ cup cold water + more if necessary

If you are going to prebake the pie crust, place an oven rack in the middle position and preheat the oven to 450° for a metal or ceramic pie pan or 425° for a glass pie pan.

Combine the flour, salt, oil and water in a medium bowl and mix well by hand with a fork or wooden spoon for about 1 minute. Shape the dough into a ball. If it won't hold together, add 1 teaspoon water.

Sprinkle 1 teaspoon flour onto a 14-inch-long sheet of wax paper. Place the ball of dough in the center and sprinkle ½ teaspoon flour over the top. Place a second 14-inch-long sheet of wax paper on top of the floured dough and, using a rolling pin, roll it into a circle approximately 12 inches across (see Mom Tip). It should be about ⅛ inch thick.

Remove and discard the top sheet of wax paper. Pick up the bottom sheet and place it, dough side down, on a 9-inch pie pan. Carefully peel off the wax paper and ease the dough into the pan. Press against the bottom and then up the sides of the pan.

Using kitchen scissors, cut off all but ½ inch of the excess dough hanging over the edge. Fold the protruding edge under itself (not under the edge of the pie pan), and press down so that it is flat against the pan rim. Using fork tines or your thumbs, press down to make an indentation. This is called fluting. Check to make sure there are no holes or cracks in the dough; patch it with extra dough if necessary.

TO PREBAKE THE CRUST: Gently poke the tines of a fork into a dozen places on the base of the crust and about every 2 inches on the sides to keep it from puffing up as it bakes. Bake for about 8 to 12 minutes, or until the crust is golden brown and crisp to the touch. Remove from the oven and cool on a rack until ready to fill. If any cracks or holes develop, patch them (see Mom Tip, page 159).

Chocolate Crumb Crust

Makes: 1 pie crust ⏱ Preparation time: 10 minutes 🔥 Baking time: 10–12 minutes for prebaking the crust ♨ Rating: Very Easy

~~~~~~

C hocolate Crumb Crust serves as another layer of chocolate in a pie—or just eat it all by itself.

⅓ cup unsalted butter + more for greasing

1½ cups chocolate graham cracker or chocolate wafer crumbs (about ⅓ package; see Mom Tip)

¼ cup sugar

✍ Mom Tip
Sixteen-ounce boxes of graham crackers usually contain 3 individually wrapped packages of crackers.

If you are going to prebake the crust, place an oven rack in the middle position and preheat the oven to 350° for a metal or ceramic pie pan or 325° for a glass pie pan.

Lightly rub the bottom and sides of a 9-inch pie pan with butter. Set aside.

Melt the butter in a small pot over low heat.

Grind the graham crackers into fine crumbs in a food processor or blender, or put them in a plastic bag and crush them with a rolling pin or heavy can. Add the sugar and melted butter to the food processor, and process for about 30 seconds, or until evenly moistened. Or transfer the crumbs to a medium bowl, add the sugar and melted butter and mix with a wooden spoon for about 1 minute, or until evenly moistened.

Transfer the crumb mixture to the pie pan. With your hands, press the crumbs firmly into the bottom of the pan and up the sides. Try to make the crust equally thick everywhere.

TO PREBAKE THE CRUST: Bake for 10 to 12 minutes, or until the crust is firm to the touch. Remove from the oven and cool on a rack until ready to fill.

Peanutty Pie Crust

Makes: 1 pie crust ⏲ Preparation time: 10 minutes ✋ Chilling time: 10 minutes 🔥 Baking time: 15–20 minutes for prebaking the crust ✋ Rating: Easy

A pie crust can just be a catchall, something to hold the filling together on its way to your mouth, or it can add a whole extra food group to the dessert. Peanutty Pie Crust counts as a vegetable.

  ¼ cup (½ stick) unsalted butter
  ¼ cup creamy peanut butter
  1 cup all-purpose flour + more for rolling
  ½ teaspoon baking powder
  ¼ teaspoon salt
  2–3 tablespoons cold water

USING A FOOD PROCESSOR: Process the butter and peanut butter about 30 seconds, or until well blended. Add the flour, baking powder and salt, and pulse about 10 times, or until the flour has been absorbed. Add 2 tablespoons water and pulse for a few seconds, or just until the dough is crumbly. Do not overprocess, or the dough will be tough. Try to pinch together some dough. If it won't stick together, add 1 more tablespoon water and pulse several times. Don't add any more water unless absolutely necessary or the dough will be too sticky.

MIXING BY HAND: Put the flour, baking powder and salt in a large bowl and stir to combine. Cut the butter into ½-inch pieces and add to the mixture. Add the peanut butter. Using a pastry cutter (see Mom Tip, page 164) or two knives, cut the butter and peanut butter into pea-size bits and toss until they are covered with the flour mixture. Add 2 tablespoons water, and mix until the dough begins to stick together. If it won't stick together, add 1 tablespoon water. Don't add any more water unless absolutely necessary or the dough will be too sticky.

Press the dough into a ball, flatten it into a 1-inch-thick disk, enclose it in a self-sealing plastic bag or plastic wrap and put it in the freezer for 10 minutes to firm the dough and make it easier to roll out.

If you are going to prebake the crust, place an oven rack in the middle position and preheat the oven to 350° for a metal or ceramic pie pan or 325° for a glass pie pan.

Sprinkle 1 teaspoon flour onto a 14-inch-long sheet of wax paper. Place the dough in the center of the wax paper and sprinkle ½ teaspoon flour over the top. Place a second 14-inch-long sheet of wax paper on top of the floured dough and, using a rolling pin, roll the dough into a circle approximately 12 inches across (see Mom Tip, page 153). It should be about ⅛ inch thick.

Remove and discard the top sheet of wax paper. Pick up the bottom sheet and place it, dough side down, on a 9-inch pie pan. Carefully peel off the wax paper and ease the dough into the pan. Press it against the bottom and then up the sides of the pan.

Using kitchen scissors, cut off all but ½ inch of the excess dough hanging over the edge. Fold the protruding edge of dough under itself (not under the edge of the pie pan), and press down so that it is flat against the pan rim. Using fork tines or your thumbs, press down to make an indentation. This is called fluting. If there are any holes or cracks in the dough, patch them with extra dough.

TO PREBAKE THE PIE CRUST: Gently poke the tines of a fork into a dozen places on the base of the crust and about every 2 inches on the sides to keep it from puffing up as it bakes. Bake for about 15 to 20 minutes, or until the crust is golden brown and crisp to the touch. If any holes or cracks develop, patch them (see Mom Tip). Remove from the oven and cool on a rack until ready to fill.

Cookie Dough Pie Crust

Makes: 1 pie crust ⓠ Preparation time: 20 minutes ✋ Chilling time: 1 hour 🔥 Baking time: 25–30 minutes for prebaking the crust 🥄 Rating: Not So Easy

~~~~~~

This crust tastes like a cookie. It's nice to have a pie crust that doesn't taste like it belongs in a quiche.

    ¼ cup slivered or sliced almonds
    6 tablespoons unsalted butter + more for greasing
    ½ cup powdered sugar
    1 large egg
    ½ teaspoon vanilla extract
 1¼ cups all-purpose flour + more for rolling
    ⅛ teaspoon salt

Mom Tip
This crust can remain
refrigerated for up to 1
week.

Place an oven rack in the middle position and preheat the oven to 325°.

Spread the almonds on a cookie sheet and bake them for about 5 minutes, or until they begin to turn golden brown. Be careful they don't burn. Set aside until cool.

Put the almonds in a food processor, and process for about 10 seconds, or until they are chopped into ⅛-inch pieces (do not overprocess or they will turn into nut butter), or chop them with a knife. Add the butter and powdered sugar to the processor, or put them in a large bowl with the almonds. Process, or beat with an electric mixer on high speed until smooth and creamy. Add the egg and vanilla, and process or beat until well blended. Add the flour and salt, and pulse for about 20 seconds or beat on low speed until combined. Do not beat too much, or the crust will be tough. Gather the dough into a ball, put it in a plastic bag and refrigerate for 1 hour (see Mom Tip).

If you are going to prebake the crust, place an oven rack in the middle position and preheat the oven to 350° for a metal or ceramic pie pan or 325° for a glass pie pan.

Lightly rub the bottom and sides of a 9-inch pie pan with butter. Set aside.

Sprinkle 1 teaspoon flour on a 14-inch-long sheet of wax paper. Place the ball of dough in the center of the wax paper and sprinkle ½ teaspoon flour over the top. Place a second 14-inch-long sheet of wax paper on top of the floured dough and, using a rolling pin, roll the dough into a circle approximately 12 inches across (see Mom Tip, page 153). It should be about ⅛ inch thick.

Remove and discard the top sheet of wax paper. Pick up the bottom sheet and place it, dough side down, on the pie pan. Carefully peel off the wax paper and ease the dough into the pan. Press it against the bottom and then up the sides of the pan.

Using kitchen scissors, cut off all but ½ inch of the excess dough hanging over the edge. Fold the protruding edge of dough under itself (not under the edge of the pie pan), and press down so that it is flat against the pan rim. Using fork tines or your thumbs, press down to make an indentation. This is called fluting. Check to make sure there are no holes or cracks in the dough; patch it with extra dough if necessary.

TO PREBAKE THE CRUST: Gently poke the tines of a fork into a dozen places on the base of the crust and about every 2 inches on the sides to keep it from puffing up as it bakes. Bake for about 25 to 30 minutes, or until the crust is golden brown and crisp to the touch. If any cracks or holes develop, patch them (see Mom Tip, page 159). Remove from the oven and cool on a rack until ready to fill.

Easy Cocoa Crust

Makes: 1 pie crust ⏰ Preparation time: 10 minutes 🔥 Baking time: 8–10 minutes for prebaking the crust ✋ Rating: Easy

By adding cocoa powder and sugar to a simple pie crust recipe, you can bring a regular crust to life. And it's nice to know you can use cocoa for more than just hot chocolate.

    1 cup all-purpose flour
    ¼ cup unsweetened cocoa powder + more for rolling
    ¼ cup sugar
    ¼ teaspoon salt
    ½ cup (1 stick) unsalted butter, cut into ½-inch pieces
    1 large egg yolk
    1 teaspoon vanilla extract

Mom Tip

A pastry cutter, which has four or five half-circles of wire attached to a handle, cuts butter into small pieces and incorporates it into a flour mixture. To use a pastry cutter, hold on to the handle and press down into the mixture until the wires touch the bottom of the bowl. Lift the cutter and press it into a different area, continuing until the butter is fully incorporated.

Mom Warning

If you sprinkle the wax paper with flour instead of cocoa, some of the flour may stick to the crust's surface and show when you transfer it to the pie plate.

If you are going to prebake the crust, place an oven rack in the middle position and preheat the oven to 350° for a metal or ceramic pie pan or 325° for a glass pie pan.

Put the flour, cocoa, sugar and salt in a food processor or a large bowl. Pulse or stir to combine. Add the butter, and process for about 20 seconds, or until fully combined. Or, using a pastry cutter (see Mom Tip) or two knives, cut into pea-size bits and toss until they are covered with the flour mixture. Add the egg yolk and vanilla, and pulse about 20 times or mix lightly with a fork, just until the dough forms itself into a ball. Do not overmix, or the pastry will be tough. Gather the dough into a ball.

Sprinkle 1 teaspoon cocoa (see Mom Warning) onto a 14-inch-long sheet of wax paper. Place the ball of dough in the center of the wax paper and sprinkle ½ teaspoon cocoa over the top. Place a second 14-inch-long sheet of wax paper on top of the dough and, using a rolling pin, roll the dough into a circle approximately 12 inches across (see Mom Tip, page 153). It should be about ⅛ inch thick.

Remove and discard the top sheet of wax paper. Pick up the bottom sheet and place it, dough side down, on a 9-inch pie pan. Carefully peel off the wax paper and ease the dough into the pan. Press it against the bottom and then up the sides of the pan.

Using kitchen scissors, cut off all but ½ inch of the excess dough hanging over the edge. Fold the protruding edge of dough under itself (not under the edge of the pie pan), and press down so that it is flat against the pan rim. Using fork tines or your thumbs, press down to make an indentation. This is called fluting. Check to make sure there are no holes or cracks in the dough; patch it with extra dough if necessary.

TO PREBAKE THE CRUST: Gently poke the tines of a fork into a dozen places on the base of the crust and about every 2 inches on the sides to keep it from puffing up as it bakes. Bake for about 8 to 10 minutes, or until the crust is golden brown and crisp to the touch. If any cracks or holes develop, patch them (Mom Tip, page 159), using cocoa instead of flour. Remove from the oven and cool on a rack until ready to fill.

Mousses/Soufflés/ Puddings

Pudding is chocolate you eat with a spoon. Even such supposedly elegant desserts as Incredibly Easy Chocolate Mousse and Foolproof Mini Chocolate Soufflés are really just puddings with an attitude. So strap on your bib, and don't hesitate to lick the bowl.

Chocolate Crème Brûlée ★ 168

Creamy Chocolate Mousse ★ 170

Incredibly Easy Chocolate Mousse ★ 172

Instant Chocolate Mousse Fix ★ 174

Low-Fat Creamy Chocolate Yogurt ★ 176

Foolproof Mini Chocolate Soufflés with
Chocolate Sauce ★ 178

Chocolate Bread Pudding ★ 181

Gooey Double-Chocolate Brownie Pudding ★ 184

Real Chocolate Pudding ★ 186

1912 Six cases of confectionery, several crates of chocolate éclairs and 1,750 quarts of ice cream, much of it chocolate, go down on the <u>Titanic</u>. While the band plays to the bitter end and upper-class men dress as ladies to sneak onto the lifeboats, the world's finest chocolate becomes the most expensive fish food ever made. News accounts of the disaster fail to mention the fate of the chocolate.

Chocolate Crème Brûlée

Serves: 8 🕐 Preparation time: 15 minutes 🔥 Baking time: 50–55 minutes ✋ Cooling time: 3–4 hours 📐 Special equipment: 8 (4-ounce) ovenproof ramekins (see Mom Tip) 👍 Rating: Easy

Mom Tip
Ovenproof ramekins are available in kitchenware shops and cost a few dollars apiece. They are useful for puddings, mini-soufflés and individual servings of fruit salad or vegetables. Those that hold ½ cup liquid are perfect for this recipe.

Anything French sounds like it must be difficult to make. But this rich custard with a crispy topping is surprisingly easy. After one taste you'll wonder why anybody would eat a nonchocolate version.

6 squares (6 ounces) bittersweet or semisweet chocolate
2 cups heavy cream
¼ cup sugar
4 egg yolks
1 teaspoon vanilla extract
½ teaspoon salt
3 tablespoons brown sugar

Place an oven rack in the middle position and preheat the oven to 300°. Fill a 9-x-13-inch roasting pan half full of water and place it on the oven rack.

Melt the chocolate in a heavy frying pan over very low heat, stirring constantly. When the chocolate is almost melted, turn off the heat and set aside to cool. The heat of the pan will melt the remaining chocolate.

Stir in the cream and the ¼ cup sugar, and mix thoroughly. If the chocolate separates into flecks, resume heating over very low heat for about 30 seconds, or until the mixture warms enough to blend the chocolate into the cream. Remove from the heat.

Remove and discard any white viscous matter attached to the egg yolks. Stir the egg yolks, vanilla and salt into the chocolate mixture and mix thoroughly.

Pour the mixture into eight 4-ounce ovenproof ramekins. Gently place the ramekins in the roasting pan; the water will come halfway up the sides.

Bake for 50 to 55 minutes, or until the crème brûlées are set. A skin will have formed on the top of each, and a knife will come out clean when inserted into the center.

Remove from the oven and cool to room temperature. Refrigerate, uncovered, for 3 to 4 hours, or until cold (see Mom Warning).

Shortly before serving, preheat the broiler, making sure the top oven rack is in the highest position, just under the broiling unit.

Place the ramekins on a baking sheet. Sprinkle about 1 teaspoon brown sugar evenly over the top of each crème brûlée. Slide the baking sheet under the broiling unit, and broil for 1 to 2 minutes, or until the sugar caramelizes.

Serve immediately or within 1 hour.

Creamy Chocolate Mousse

Serves: 8 Preparation time: 15 minutes Baking time: None Cooling time: 30 minutes
Rating: Very Easy

This easy recipe substitutes cream for the usual raw eggs. When I'm beating the cream, I do feel a little like an eighteenth-century pioneer woman churning butter outside my log cabin. But a little role-playing is healthy in life.

 8 squares (8 ounces) semisweet chocolate
 ½ cup milk
 1 tablespoon Kahlúa, Cointreau or raspberry liqueur
 1 cup heavy cream
  Fresh raspberries or strawberries (optional)

Melt the chocolate in a heavy frying pan over very low heat, stirring constantly. When the chocolate is almost melted, turn off the heat and set aside to cool. The heat of the pan will melt the remaining chocolate.

Mom Tip
Put the empty bowl and beaters in the freezer for 10 minutes before using them. Cream will whip faster if the bowl and the beaters are ice cold.

Stir in the milk and the liqueur and mix until fully incorporated. Set aside.

Pour the cream into a medium bowl, and beat with an electric mixer until it thickens (see Mom Tip), 1 to 2 minutes. Pour the chocolate mixture over the cream and mix them gently with a rubber spatula, scooping up the cream from the bottom of the bowl and turning the spatula over repeatedly until no white is showing. Pour the mixture evenly among eight small dishes or into one serving bowl. Cover with plastic wrap and refrigerate for at least 30 minutes. The mousse will thicken as it cools. Serve plain or with a few raspberries or strawberries, if you like. Store leftovers, covered, in the refrigerator.

Incredibly Easy Chocolate Mousse

Serves: 6 ✆ Preparation time: 10 minutes 🐝 Baking time: None ✋ Cooling time: 1 hour or overnight ✎ Special equipment: Blender ✎ Rating: Very Easy

I've always thought of chocolate mousse as something very special, because my mom would only make it on very special occasions, such as funerals. Now that I'm older, I realize that no one has to die for me to enjoy Chocolate Mousse. All I need is a blender and a few free minutes.

☼! Mom Warning
This dessert contains raw eggs.

☞ Mom Tip
Crème de Cacao, Kahlúa and Grand Marnier are available in tiny bottles.

  1 cup (6-ounce package) semisweet chocolate chips
⅓ cup very hot coffee or 1 teaspoon instant coffee granules
      dissolved in ⅓ cup boiling water
  4 large eggs (see Mom Warning)
  2 tablespoons vanilla extract, Crème de Cacao, Kahlúa or
      Grand Marnier (see Mom Tip)
     Whipped cream (page 275; optional)

Put the chocolate chips in the blender and pour the hot coffee over them. Cover, and blend on high speed for about 15 seconds, or until the mixture is very smooth. Scrape down the sides with a rubber spatula and blend again for a few seconds.

Separate the eggs, putting the egg whites into a large metal or ceramic bowl with no traces of grease and the egg yolks into the chocolate mixture. Set the whites aside. Add the vanilla or liqueur to the chocolate mixture, cover and blend on high speed for about 15 seconds, or until the mixture is thick and smooth.

Beat the egg whites with an electric mixer just until they form stiff peaks. Do not overbeat.

Pour the chocolate mixture over the beaten egg whites and mix them gently with a rubber spatula, scooping up egg white from the bottom of the bowl and turning the spatula over repeatedly until no white is showing. Pour the mousse evenly among six small dishes or into one serving bowl. Cover with plastic wrap and refrigerate for at least 1 hour or overnight. Serve plain or with whipped cream, if you like. Store leftovers, covered, in the refrigerator.

Instant Chocolate Mousse Fix

Serves: 4 Preparation time: 5 minutes Special equipment: Food processor or blender
Rating: Very Easy

I'm always on the lookout for ways to satisfy my midnight cravings for chocolate. For years, I would make chocolate chip cookie batter and eat it right out of the food processor. Then I found this recipe. Mixing chocolate with ricotta cheese took a leap of faith, but now I have a great new way to get that five-minute fix.

This is our agent's recipe, so when you're done cooking, put fifteen percent of it in an envelope and send it to her.

2 cups skim-milk ricotta cheese

¾ cup unsweetened cocoa powder

¾ cup sugar

1 tablespoon milk + more if needed

1 teaspoon vanilla extract, Crème de Cacao, Kahlúa or Grand Marnier (see Mom Tip, page 172)

Combine all the ingredients in a food processor or blender, and process for several minutes, or until smooth. Add another tablespoon of milk if the mousse is too thick.

Divide the mixture evenly among four small dishes or pour it into one serving bowl. Serve immediately, or cover and refrigerate until needed.

Low-Fat Creamy Chocolate Yogurt

Serves: 8　Preparation time: 10 minutes　Special equipment: Food processor or blender　Rating: Very Easy

Chocolate yogurt was one of my favorite snacks in England, where I grew up. Recently, I learned how to make my own—and now you can, too, instead of settling for those bland fruit-on-the-bottom yogurts.

Mom Tip
Start with 2 tablespoons sugar. If the yogurt isn't sweet enough, add more sugar, 1 teaspoon at a time. Kevin and I prefer 2 tablespoons plus 1 teaspoon sugar.

1 cup low-fat cottage cheese
1 cup plain yogurt
½ cup unsweetened cocoa powder
¼ cup maple syrup
2 tablespoons sugar or more, depending on your taste (see Mom Tip)
1 teaspoon vanilla extract

Combine all the ingredients in the bowl of a food processor or blender, and process for about 1 minute, or until the mixture is smooth. Pour evenly among eight small serving dishes or into one serving bowl. Serve immediately, or cover and refrigerate until needed.

Foolproof Mini Chocolate Soufflés with Chocolate Sauce

Serves: 4 ⏲ Preparation time: 20 minutes 🔥 Baking time: 20–25 minutes ♟ Rating: Easy

I've heard stories of French chefs who would commit suicide if their soufflé fell. That sounds far-fetched to me. Something else must have been bothering them. Mom has made this recipe as easy as possible, in case you're teetering on the edge and a soufflé mishap would send you over it. And if the soufflé does fall a little bit, you can fill the divot with chocolate sauce. Either way, you're covered.

🖝 Mom Tip 1
If you don't have individual soufflé dishes, you can use oven-proof coffee cups (but not mugs).

🖝 Mom Tip 2
To help get the soufflé dishes out of the oven easily, bake them on a cookie sheet and then simply lift the cookie sheet out of the oven.

½ cup sugar + 4 teaspoons for coating
8 squares (8 ounces) semisweet chocolate
3 large eggs
1 teaspoon vanilla extract
½ cup heavy cream

Place an oven rack in the middle position and preheat the oven to 400°. Lightly rub four individual soufflé dishes (see Mom Tip 1) with butter. Put 1 teaspoon sugar in each dish, and tilt the dish so that the buttered surfaces are covered with sugar. Use more sugar if necessary. Set aside (see Mom Tip 2).

Melt the chocolate in a heavy frying pan over very low heat, stirring constantly. When the chocolate is almost melted, turn off the heat and set aside to cool. The heat of the pan will melt the remaining chocolate.

Separate the eggs, putting the whites into a medium metal or ceramic bowl with no traces of grease, and the yolks in another medium bowl. Set the egg yolks aside.

Beat the egg whites with an electric mixer just until they form stiff peaks. Do not overbeat. Set aside.

Add the ½ cup sugar and vanilla to the yolks and beat with an electric mixer or a whisk for about 1 minute, or until thick and light yellow.

Add half the melted chocolate to the beaten yolk mixture. Set aside the rest of the chocolate for making the sauce. Stir the chocolate mixture thoroughly. Add the beaten egg whites and fold them together gently with a rubber spatula, turning the mixture over repeatedly until no white is showing.

Pour the mixture evenly among the four prepared soufflé dishes. Bake for 20 to 25 minutes, or until the mini soufflés have risen and are beginning to brown. Remove from the oven.

To make the sauce: While the mini soufflés are baking, add the cream to the reserved melted chocolate and stir thoroughly to incorporate. If the chocolate is too firm, heat it for about 1 minute over very low heat, stirring constantly, until it softens enough to combine with the cream.

Unlike most soufflés, which must be served as soon as they come out of the oven, these mini soufflés can wait to be served for up to 30 minutes. Their tops will fall a little, but no one will notice because, just before serving, you make an incision in the top of each one with a knife, and then spoon in about 2 tablespoons of the warm chocolate sauce. And if the soufflé hasn't fully cooked, no one will notice, because of the added sauce. Store leftovers, covered, in the refrigerator.

1923 A Hershey employee, H. B. Reese, founds his own company. Inspired by his boss's success, Reese hopes there's room on the gravy train for him. He quits his job and retreats to
his kitchen, where he concocts a variety of such questionable candies as chocolate-covered dates and
coconut caramel bars. He has no success until 1941, when wartime sugar rationing forces him to
focus on the Peanut Butter Cup. Deprivation should always have such consequences.

Chocolate Bread Pudding

Serves: 4–6 Preparation time: 25 minutes Baking time: 35–40 minutes Waiting time:
30 minutes Chilling time: (4 hours, if you prefer it cold) Rating: Easy

In England, all dessert is called "pudding." Even if it's apple pie à la mode, it's pudding. This is confusing, because sometimes English pudding is actually pudding—this one, for instance. The recipe comes from my mom's friend Judy Rich, a Londoner who is actually a transplanted American. A true chocolate-lover, she knows that no one can live "by bread alone."

Mom Tip
The better the bread, the better the pudding. Bakery bread left over from a dinner party works very well, even if it's slightly stale. You can also use day-old French bread; but instead of 6 slices, use 12, since they're so small.

4 squares (4 ounces) semisweet chocolate

¼ cup (½ stick) unsalted butter + more for greasing

6 ¼-inch-thick slices best-quality white bread (see Mom Tip)

1¼ cups heavy cream

⅓ cup sugar

2 large eggs

2 teaspoons vanilla extract

Chocolate Syrup (page 236; optional)

Melt the chocolate and butter in a heavy frying pan over very low heat, stirring occasionally. When the chocolate is almost melted, turn off the heat and set aside to cool. The heat of the pot will melt the remaining chocolate. Meanwhile, cut the slices of bread into quarters. Set aside.

Add the cream and sugar to the melted chocolate mixture, and mix well. Beat the eggs and the vanilla together in a small bowl. Add to the chocolate mixture, and stir until the custard is smooth.

Wipe the bottom and sides of a 1-quart ovenproof casserole with butter. Spoon 3 to 4 tablespoons of the custard into the casserole and spread it around with the back of a spoon. Arrange half the bread slices over the custard, overlapping them slightly. Spoon half of the custard over the bread layer, and repeat with the remaining bread and custard. Let sit at room temperature for at least 30 minutes, so that the bread absorbs the custard and becomes soggy.

About 15 minutes before you want to bake the pudding, place an oven rack in the middle position and preheat the oven to 350°.

Bake for 35 to 40 minutes, or until the top is beginning to brown. Remove from the oven and spoon the pudding into small bowls. Or if you prefer to serve it cold, cool to room temperature. Then cover and refrigerate for at least 4 hours or overnight.

If you are serving the pudding with chocolate syrup, put the syrup in a serving bowl or pitcher, and offer it separately.

1926 Godiva Chocolate Company is founded in Belgium, with the image of a nude woman riding a horse as its logo. The figure is based on the legendary eleventh-century noblewoman Lady Godiva, who rode her horse naked through the English town of Coventry to promote lower taxes for the poor. Apparently her effort was successful. Maybe the next time Congress debates the tax code, it should forget filibusters and head to the stables.

Gooey Double-Chocolate Brownie Pudding

Serves: 8 Preparation time: 30 minutes Baking time: 35–40 minutes Rating: Very Easy

The name of this recipe says it all. Just leave your manners with the neighbors, and grab a shovel to eat it with.

- ½ cup (1 stick) unsalted butter + more for greasing
- 1 square (1 ounce) unsweetened chocolate
- ¾ cup sugar
- 1 cup all-purpose flour
- 2 teaspoons baking powder
- ¼ teaspoon salt
- ½ cup milk
- 1 teaspoon vanilla extract
- 1 cup chopped walnuts (optional)

☼! Mom Warning
Not mixing the brownie batter and the cocoa liquid is what creates a dessert that is part pudding and part cake.

¼ cup unsweetened cocoa powder

½ cup brown sugar

1 cup hot water

   Vanilla ice cream

Place an oven rack in the middle position and preheat the oven to 350°. Lightly rub an 8- or 9-inch square pan with butter. Set aside.

Melt the chocolate and butter in a small, heavy pot over very low heat, stirring occasionally. When the chocolate is almost melted, turn off the heat and set aside to cool. The heat of the pot will melt the remaining chocolate.

Combine the sugar, flour, baking powder and salt in a large mixing bowl. Stir in the milk, vanilla and chocolate mixture and mix well. If using walnuts, mix them in now. Pour the mixture into the pan and spread it evenly.

Combine the cocoa, brown sugar and hot water in a small bowl, mix well and pour over the top of the cake mixture. Do *not* mix together (see Mom Warning).

Bake for 35 to 40 minutes, or until the top of the cake feels firm to the touch. Remove from the oven and cut into 8 pieces. Transfer to bowls, turning the pieces upside down so that the pudding underneath shows. Serve warm with a small scoop of vanilla ice cream. Store leftovers, covered, in the refrigerator.

Real Chocolate Pudding

Serves: 8 ⏲ Preparation time: 25 minutes ✋ Cooling time: 5 minutes (warm); 30 minutes (room temperature) ♨ Rating: Easy

In college, after eating a well-balanced meal of scrod and mashed potatoes at the dining hall, I would return to the table with about ten little containers of chocolate pudding. My friends would watch in astonishment as I polished them all off. I wouldn't have looked so gluttonous if the containers had been larger. Now that I'm more mature, I can cook my own pudding and eat it out of the pot. It's almost as easy as taking the tops off all those containers.

4 squares (4 ounces) bittersweet or semisweet chocolate
1 large egg + 2 large yolks
⅓ cup sugar
3 tablespoons unsweetened cocoa powder
7 teaspoons (2⅓ tablespoons) cornstarch

Mom Tip 1
I prefer nonfat milk in this recipe, because the pudding is rich enough as it is. However, you can use whole or part-skim milk, if you prefer.

Mom Tip 2
To prevent a skin from forming on the top of the pudding as it cools, press a layer of plastic wrap right onto the surface of the pudding.

1 teaspoon instant coffee granules

¼ teaspoon salt

2 cups nonfat milk (see Mom Tip 1)

2 tablespoons unsalted butter

1 teaspoon vanilla extract

Whipped cream (page 275; optional)

Melt the chocolate in a small, heavy pot over very low heat, stirring constantly. When the chocolate is almost melted, turn off the heat and set aside to cool. The heat of the pot will melt the remaining chocolate.

Put the egg and yolks in a medium, heavy pot, and beat for a few seconds with a fork. Add the sugar, cocoa, cornstarch, coffee granules and salt, and mix until thoroughly combined.

Stir in the milk and begin heating over medium heat, stirring continually. Cook for about 5 minutes, or until bubbles form around the edges and the mixture begins to thicken. Add the melted chocolate, butter and vanilla, and stir to incorporate. Remove from the heat, and spoon the mixture evenly among eight small bowls or into a large serving bowl. Serve warm, at room temperature or cold (see Mom Tip 2). Serve with whipped cream, if you like. Store leftovers, covered, in the refrigerator.

Chocolate with Fruit/ Ice Cream

To some people, fruit is a dessert by itself. These are the kindly folks who stand in the doorway handing out apples on Halloween and then can't understand why the bushes in their yard are crisscrossed with toilet paper in the morning. To those possessed by chocolate, nature's goodness just ain't good enough. Luckily, you can have your fruit, and chocolate, too.

Ice cream tastes just fine by itself (unless it's that low-fat stuff that's more like ice crystals). But you can give it a twist to make it serve a higher chocolate purpose. Desserts such as Mississippi Mud Pie show that ice cream can be more inspiring than sitting at the kitchen table in the middle of the night and eating out of the carton.

Frozen Chocolate Banana Slices/
    Chocolate-Dipped Apricots ★ 190
Chocolate Fondue ★ 192
Chocolate Dessert Crêpes ★ 195
Chocolate Strawberry Shortcake ★ 199
Peachy Chocolate Chip Crisp ★ 202
Fresh Strawberry Meringues Drizzled with
    Chocolate ★ 204
Raspberry Chocolate Pudding Cake ★ 206
Fabulous Four Seasons Banana Cake ★ 208

Raspberry Chocolate Tart ★ 211
Cherry-Chocolate Truffle Pie ★ 215
Chocolate Strawberry Pie ★ 217
Chocolate Pizza ★ 219

Minty Ice Cream Sandwiches ★ 223
Chocolate Profiteroles ★ 226
Mississippi Mud Pie ★ 228

1930 In a twist of fate, the chocolate chip cookie is invented before the chocolate chip. Ruth Wakefield, owner of the Toll House Inn in Whitman, Massachusetts, cuts a brick of chocolate into small pieces and adds them to her cookie dough. The cookies become very popular with her guests, and soon men from Nestlé with dark sunglasses and briefcases handcuffed to their wrists stop in and make her a proposition. In the 1940s, Mrs. Wakefield sells all rights to the Toll House trademark to Nestlé.

Frozen Chocolate Banana Slices/ Chocolate-Dipped Apricots

Serves: 4 Preparation time: 20 minutes Chilling time: 30 minutes Rating: Very Easy

When my family moved to L.A. in 1980, one of the first places we went was Disneyland. The vivid memories of that trip were my sister running in terror from a man dressed as Captain Hook and me stuffing my face with frozen chocolate bananas. While my sister is still in therapy to make the nightmares go away, I've been back to Disneyland a dozen times to eat those bananas. Forget the rides.

When trying to make frozen bananas at home, we found it was very difficult to dip a whole banana in chocolate. So we went with the slices. They taste just as good — and it's harder to keep track of how many you've eaten.

Mom Tip
Orange sections,
strawberries, dried
figs and pretzels are
also good dipped in
chocolate. Follow the
directions given above
for the apricots.

6 squares (6 ounces) semisweet or bittersweet chocolate

4 small bananas or 6 ripe apricots or 16 dried apricots

Melt the chocolate in a heavy frying pan over very low heat, stirring constantly. When the chocolate is almost melted, turn off the heat and set aside to cool. The heat of the pan will melt the remaining chocolate.

Place a large sheet of wax paper on a cookie sheet. Set aside.

If using bananas, peel and slice them into ½-inch slices. Immerse a banana slice in the melted chocolate with a fork. Carefully remove it from the chocolate and place it on the wax paper. Repeat until all the banana slices have been dipped. Freeze them for 30 minutes, or until the chocolate has completely hardened. If you are not serving them immediately, transfer them to a heavy-duty, self-sealing plastic bag and store them in the freezer until needed. Serve frozen.

If using fresh apricots, cut them in half and discard the pits. Place the dried apricots in a bowl. Dip the fresh apricot halves or dried apricots in the melted chocolate, immersing two-thirds of the fruit. Place the dipped pieces on the wax paper to harden.

Refrigerate the fruit for 30 minutes, or until the chocolate has completely hardened. Then cover the fruit with foil or plastic wrap so that it doesn't dry out, and refrigerate until just before serving.

Chocolate Fondue

Serves: 4–6 ⏱ Preparation time: 15 minutes 🔥 Cooking time: 10 minutes ＼ Special equipment: Fondue pot + recommended fuel (see Mom Tip 1) 🔥 Rating: Very Easy

Mom Tip 1
A traditional fondue pot is made of cast iron or stainless steel. It comes with a frame and burner attachment that allows you to cook at the table. Be sure to read the fondue pot directions carefully and have on hand the recommended fuel. If you can't locate a fondue pot, substitute a small pot that sits on a hot tray, or an electric frying pan set on low heat.

Learning to share is one of the big lessons of childhood. But when it comes to chocolate, I still have trouble with the concept. Chocolate fondue forces you to share. However, everyone in my family eats as fast as possible in order to keep the sharing to a minimum.

We've given you various options, so that if you decide to make this fondue frequently, it won't taste the same each time.

CHOOSE 3 OR 4 FROM THE FOLLOWING FOR DIPPING
Banana slices
Orange sections
Peach slices
Pineapple chunks

Raspberries
Strawberries (cut in half if very large)
Angel food cake, cut into bite-size cubes
Marshmallows

Basic Chocolate Fondue

12 squares (12 ounces) semisweet, bittersweet or milk
   chocolate (see Mom Tip 2)
½ cup heavy cream
2 tablespoons brandy or 1 teaspoon vanilla extract

Chocolate Mint Fondue

12 squares (12 ounces) semisweet or bittersweet chocolate
   (see Mom Tip 2)
½ cup heavy cream
1 teaspoon peppermint extract

Chocolate Mocha Fondue

12 squares (12 ounces) semisweet or bittersweet chocolate
   (see Mom Tip 2)
½ cup heavy cream
2 tablespoons Kahlúa or 1 teaspoon vanilla extract
1 teaspoon instant coffee granules

Peanut Butter and Chocolate Fondue

12 squares (12 ounces) semisweet or bittersweet chocolate
   (see Mom Tip 2)
½ cup heavy cream
½ cup creamy peanut butter
1 teaspoon vanilla extract

✍ Mom Tip 2
Chocolate bars or
semisweet baking
chocolate works well
for fondue.

Set up the fondue pot frame and burner attachment on the table, and prepare but do not light the burner. If you have fondue forks (extra-long forks with heatproof handles), set them out. You can also use regular forks, metal skewers or chopsticks.

Arrange the fruit and/or cake and marshmallows in small bowls or plates and set on the table.

Break the chocolate into small pieces and place in the fondue pot. Add the cream (or peanut butter) and brandy or vanilla (or peppermint extract or Kahlúa and coffee granules) and place on the stove over low heat. Stir constantly until the chocolate has melted and the mixture is smooth. Do not let it boil.

Light the burner attachment. Bring the fondue pot to the table and set it over the burner.

Chocolate Dessert Crêpes

Serves: 6 ⏲ Preparation time: 20 minutes ✋ Waiting time: 30 minutes 🔥 Cooking time: 20 minutes (1½ minutes per crêpe) ☝ Rating: Not So Easy

When I was growing up in England, my dad took my sister and me to a French ski resort. The short-tempered instructor, who spoke no English, screamed at us in French as we snowplowed down vertical slopes. Dad would pick us up at the end of the afternoon and take us to a crêpe stand, so we could ruin our appetites with chocolate crêpes. It almost made the whole trip worthwhile.

Making crêpes at home can be tricky. It's difficult to flip them in the pan without their falling apart. My ratio is about one perfect crêpe to nine very imperfect ones, but I'm still practicing. The good thing is that even when they don't turn out exactly round, they still taste great.

Mom Tip
Nutella is chocolate-hazelnut spread. It's available in jars in gourmet stores and many supermarkets, usually near the baking chocolate. It has the consistency of creamy peanut butter. If you can't find it, use Ganache (page 70).

CRÊPES

¾ cup milk

2 large eggs

½ cup all-purpose flour

¼ cup sugar

2 tablespoons unsweetened cocoa powder

1 teaspoon vanilla extract

2 tablespoons unsalted butter + more if needed

FILLING

1 large or 2 small bananas, sliced into ¼-inch-thick rounds, or 12 strawberries, sliced ¼ inch thick

½ cup Nutella + more if needed (see Mom Tip)

6 tablespoons Cointreau or Grand Marnier, or 1 teaspoon powdered sugar

TO MAKE THE CRÊPES: Put the milk, eggs, flour, sugar, cocoa and vanilla in a blender or a large bowl. Process, or beat with an electric mixer on low speed until well blended and frothy. Cover the mixture, and set aside for 30 minutes so that it will thicken slightly.

TO COOK THE CRÊPES: Set out a large plate and lay a sheet of wax paper on it. Prepare 10 more sheets of wax paper. Cut the butter into 13 small pieces. Set out a ¼-cup measure.

Blend or stir the batter for a few seconds so that it is mixed through.

Begin heating a crêpe pan or small (8-inch) frying pan over medium heat. Add 1 piece of butter and swirl it around so that it melts and fully coats the pan.

When the butter begins to sizzle, fill the ¼-cup measure half full of batter, pour it into the pan and quickly tip the pan in all directions so that the batter spreads out in a thin layer as it begins to cook. Cook for about 30 seconds, or until the crêpe is firm on the underside and the top looks almost cooked. Loosen the edges with a metal spatula and then slide the spatula under part of the crêpe. If it sticks, jerk the pan back and forth to try to loosen it.

Turn the crêpe over gently with the spatula, using your fingers to help, if necessary, and cook for another 10 to 15 seconds. Carefully transfer the crêpe to the plate, making sure it lies flat. Don't be surprised if the first one is a disaster. Throw it out and start again; the others will turn out better.

Add another piece of butter to the pan and repeat until you've finished the batter, putting a layer of wax paper on top of each crêpe as you stack them (see Mom Warning). This amount of batter will make between 12 and 15 crêpes, depending on how big your pan is.

You can make the crêpes early in the day and store them, wax paper included, in a self-sealing plastic bag in the refrigerator.

About 15 minutes before you want to serve the crêpes, place an oven rack in the middle position and preheat the oven to 350°.

To FILL THE CRÊPES: Put each crêpe on its piece of wax paper on the counter and spread each with 1 teaspoon of the Nutella. Place 4 banana or strawberry slices in the center. Fold each crêpe in half and then in half again, so that it is shaped like a triangle. Place them on an oven-to-table platter so that they overlap slightly, and heat in the oven for 7 to 10 minutes, or until the Nutella is hot. Don't leave them in too long or the crêpes will dry out.

To serve from the platter, pour the liqueur over the crêpes or sprinkle them with the powdered sugar, using a sieve. To serve individually, transfer 2 crêpes to each plate. Spoon 1 tablespoon of the liqueur over each set of crêpes or sprinkle them with the powdered sugar. Serve immediately.

1940 Solving one of the perennial chocolate problems, Forrest Mars invents M&M's, a chocolate candy that won't melt in your pocket or in your hand. They're an immediate success. Mars, the estranged son of Franklin Mars, the creator of Milky Way, Snickers and Three Musketeers, is famous for his type A personality and goes into a tirade if he finds an M&M without the "m" perfectly centered. While Forrest could probably have used a long vacation, his invention becomes the cornerstone of his candy empire.

Chocolate Strawberry Shortcake

Serves: 8 ☖ Preparation time: 30 minutes ✋ Waiting time: 1 hour 🔥 Baking time: 10 minutes
⚓ Rating: Easy

~~~~~~

*S*trawberry shortcake is a classic American dessert, but what it's short of is chocolate. We've seen to that.

STRAWBERRY SAUCE
   3 pints fresh strawberries
   ½ cup sugar

SHORTCAKE

> 6 tablespoons unsalted butter, softened to room temperature
> 1¾ cups all-purpose flour + 1 teaspoon for rolling
> 2 tablespoons sugar
> 2 tablespoons unsweetened cocoa powder
> 2 teaspoons baking powder
> ½ teaspoon salt
> ¾ cup buttermilk
> 1 teaspoon vanilla extract
> 1 cup (6-ounce package) semisweet chocolate chips

> Vanilla ice cream or whipped cream (page 275; optional)

TO MAKE THE SAUCE: Rinse the strawberries and remove and discard the stems. Cut them lengthwise into ⅛-inch slices and put them in a medium bowl. Add the sugar and stir gently to coat them. Set aside at room temperature for up to 1 hour to let the strawberry juices develop. Stir occasionally. Refrigerate until needed.

TO MAKE THE SHORTCAKE: Place an oven rack in the middle position and preheat the oven to 425°. Set out a cookie sheet, but do not grease it.

Cut the butter into ½-inch pieces and put it in a food processor or a large bowl. Process, or beat with an electric mixer until smooth and creamy. Add the flour, sugar, cocoa, baking powder and salt, and pulse about 20 times or beat just until well blended. Add the buttermilk, vanilla and chocolate chips, and pulse about 15 times or beat just until the dough begins to come together in a ball. Do not beat the batter too much, or the shortcake will be tough.

Mom Tip
If you don't have a
cookie cutter, use a
cup or glass with a
2- or 3-inch diameter.
Dip the rim into flour
before pressing it
into the dough, to
keep the dough from
sticking.

Sprinkle 1 teaspoon flour over a 12-inch sheet of wax paper. Place the ball of dough in the center of the wax paper and flatten slightly with the heel of your hand. Place another sheet of wax paper on top, and roll the dough out until it is ½ inch thick. Remove the top sheet of wax paper. Set aside.

Using a cookie cutter (see Mom Tip), cut the dough into circles and place them on the cookie sheet. Gather the dough remnants and pat them together. Cover with the reserved wax paper and roll the dough out again until it is ½ inch thick. Cut as many more circles as you can and transfer them to the cookie sheet.

Bake for about 10 minutes, or until the shortcakes have risen, are firm to the touch and are beginning to brown. Remove from the oven and transfer to a rack to cool.

Serve warm or at room temperature. Split each shortcake in half through the middle and put the bottom layers in bowls. Spoon on some strawberries and juice. Place the top half of each shortcake on the strawberry layer, and spoon on more strawberries. Serve with vanilla ice cream or whipped cream, if you like.

1940 White chocolate is created in Switzerland. Having been the leaders in chocolate innovation since the invention of milk chocolate in 1875, the Swiss put an end to their winning streak by making chocolate without any chocolate in it. They should have quit while they were ahead.

Peachy Chocolate Chip Crisp

Serves: 4 ⏰ Preparation time: 20 minutes 🔥 Baking time: 30 minutes 🥄 Rating: Very Easy

Peach and chocolate is not a taste combination that seems natural at first. But it really grows on you. I promise not to try to talk you into making Broccoli Chocolate Chip Crisp.

☞ **Mom Tip**
Wheat germ, which is available in jars or packages in the cereal aisle or in health food stores, gives the topping extra crunch.

4 large or 6 medium peaches
2 tablespoons sugar
3 tablespoons unsalted butter
¼ cup all-purpose flour
¼ cup toasted wheat germ (see Mom Tip)
3 tablespoons brown sugar
1 tablespoon unsweetened cocoa powder
½ cup semisweet chocolate chips

Place an oven rack in the middle position and preheat the oven to 375°.

Bring a large pot of water to a boil over high heat. Drop in the peaches and let them cook for 1 minute to loosen their skins. Remove from the water, using a slotted spoon, and cool for a few minutes. Cut them in half and discard the pits. Pull off and discard the skins. Cut the peaches into thin slices and put in an ungreased 1-quart ovenproof casserole or 9-inch pie pan. Sprinkle with the sugar, and stir. Set aside.

Cut the butter into pea-size bits, and put in a medium bowl. Add the flour, wheat germ, brown sugar and cocoa, and toss gently. Spoon the butter-flour mixture evenly over the peaches. Sprinkle the chocolate chips on the top.

Bake for about 30 minutes, or until the peach juices bubble and the topping is crisp. The chocolate chips will retain their chip shape but will collapse when touched by a spoon.

Remove from the oven and serve immediately. Or cool, and serve at room temperature or cold.

Fresh Strawberry Meringues Drizzled with Chocolate

Serves: 4 ⏱ Preparation time: 20 minutes + 10 minutes for the fudge sauce 🔥 Baking time: 45 minutes ✋ Cooling time: 90 minutes ⚖ Rating: Very Easy

~~~~~~

When combined with strawberries and chocolate, meringues make a classy dessert—the kind you eat with a napkin in your lap.

☞ Mom Tip 1
You can substitute fresh raspberries or slices of kiwi for the strawberries.

1 large egg white
⅛ teaspoon salt
⅛ teaspoon cider vinegar
¼ cup sugar
½ teaspoon vanilla extract
8 fresh strawberries (see Mom Tip 1)
½ cup Hot Fudge Sauce (page 238; see Mom Tip 2)

Mom Tip 2
Here's how to make an even easier chocolate topping. Melt 1 cup chocolate chips or 3 squares (3 ounces) semisweet or bittersweet chocolate in a small, heavy pot over very low heat, stirring constantly. When the chocolate is almost melted, turn off the heat and stir until all the chocolate has melted. Pour it over the strawberries and serve.

Mom Tip 3
If you want these meringues to taste chocolatey, add 1 teaspoon unsweetened cocoa powder when you add the sugar.

Place an oven rack in the middle position and preheat the oven to 275°. Place a 12-inch piece of wax paper on a cookie sheet. Set aside.

Put the egg white in a small bowl with no traces of grease. Add the salt and vinegar. Beat with an electric mixer just until the egg white forms stiff peaks. Do not overbeat. Gently beat in the sugar, 2 tablespoons at a time, until all the sugar has been absorbed, 1 to 2 minutes (see Mom Tip 3). Then beat in the vanilla.

Roughly divide the mixture into fourths and spoon each fourth onto a separate area of the wax paper. Using the back of a spoon, shape each meringue into a 3-inch circle. Hollow out the middle of each one with the spoon and build up the sides, so that each meringue looks like a small soup bowl.

Bake for about 45 minutes, or until the meringues are light golden. Turn off the oven, and cool for 1 hour in the oven with the door closed.

Meanwhile, remove and discard the stems of the strawberries. Cut the berries lengthwise into ⅛-inch slices, and put in a small bowl. Set aside.

When the meringues are finished cooling, remove from the oven. Gently loosen the wax paper from the cookie sheet. If it's stuck, slide a metal or plastic spatula gently under the paper to loosen it. Once the paper is loose, peel each meringue gently away. The meringues are very delicate and easily broken, so be careful. If you are not going to use them immediately, store them in a self-sealing plastic bag at room temperature for up to 3 days.

To serve, place the meringues on small plates. Fill the centers with the sliced strawberries and pour some Hot Fudge Sauce over them.

Raspberry Chocolate Pudding Cake

Serves: 12–16 ⏰ Preparation time: 30 minutes 🔥 Baking time: 20–25 minutes ♨ Rating: Easy

My mother discovered this concoction by accident while attempting to make a raspberry cake. It may not be up there with the accidental discovery of penicillin, but I was pretty impressed. It's more moist than your average cake, but all that means is that you eat it with a spoon instead of a fork.

¾ cup slivered or sliced almonds
4 squares (4 ounces) semisweet chocolate
2 squares (2 ounces) unsweetened chocolate
¾ cup (1½ sticks) unsalted butter + more for greasing
1½ cups sugar
3 large eggs
1 teaspoon vanilla extract
1 cup all-purpose flour

½ teaspoon baking powder

¼ teaspoon salt

2 cups fresh or frozen raspberries (see Mom Tip)
Vanilla ice cream (optional)

Place an oven rack in the middle position and preheat the oven to 350°. Lightly rub a 9-x-13-inch pan with butter. Set aside.

Spread the almonds on a cookie sheet and bake for about 5 minutes, or until they begin to turn golden brown. Be careful they don't burn. Remove them from the oven and, when cool, grind in a food processor or blender or put them on a cutting board and chop them.

Melt both kinds of chocolate and the butter in a heavy frying pan over very low heat, stirring occasionally. When the chocolate is almost melted, turn off the heat and set aside to cool. The heat of the pan will melt the remaining chocolate.

Put the sugar, eggs and vanilla in a large bowl, and beat with an electric mixer or a wooden spoon until smooth and creamy. Add the melted chocolate and mix until well incorporated. Add the flour, almonds, baking powder and salt and mix just until blended.

If using fresh raspberries, rinse well and pat dry with paper towels. If using frozen raspberries, don't defrost them, but shake off any ice crystals. Gently stir the raspberries into the cake mixture.

Pour the batter into the pan, and spread evenly. Bake for 20 to 25 minutes, or until the top of the cake feels almost firm to the touch. Remove from the oven and cool on a rack for 30 minutes. Cut into pieces and transfer to bowls. Serve warm, with a dollop of vanilla ice cream, if you like. Store leftovers, covered, in the refrigerator.

Fabulous Four Seasons Banana Cake

Serves: 16 Preparation time: 40 minutes + 10 minutes for the glaze Baking time: 50–55 minutes
Cooling time: 1 hour Special equipment: 9-cup bundt pan (see Mom Tip 1) Rating: Easy

Mom Tip 1
Bundt pans are like angel food cake pans in that they have a metal tube in the middle, which means the cake will have an open space in the middle. Bundt pans also have ridges, curved shapes or other patterns embossed in the bottom. To get the cake out in one piece, be sure to generously butter and flour the pan before spooning in the cake batter.

When we first got this recipe from the Four Seasons Hotel, it called for 24 bananas and 24 eggs. Only the largest primates can consume that many bananas at a time. The recipe turned out to be for eight cakes, and Mom was able to cut it down to a more manageable human size.

⅔ cup pecans or walnuts
1½ cups (3 sticks) unsalted butter, softened to room
       temperature, + more for greasing
1 cup sugar
1 cup brown sugar
3 bananas
3 large eggs

1½ cups all-purpose flour + 2 teaspoons for dusting
1 teaspoon baking soda
½ teaspoon salt
3 tablespoons buttermilk
½ teaspoon vanilla extract
Easy Chocolate Glaze (page 66)

Place an oven rack in the middle position and preheat the oven to 350°.

Spread the pecans or walnuts on a cookie sheet, and bake for about 5 minutes, or until they begin to turn golden brown. Be careful they don't burn. Remove from the oven. When they are cool, chop them.

Generously rub the bottom and sides of a 9-cup bundt pan with butter. Add 2 teaspoons flour and swirl it around, coating the buttered surfaces. Set aside.

Put the butter and the sugars in a large bowl, and beat with an electric mixer on high speed or with a wooden spoon until smooth and creamy. Cut the bananas in chunks, add to the butter-sugar mixture and mix until well incorporated. Add the eggs, one at a time, and mix until well incorporated. Add the flour, baking soda, salt, buttermilk and vanilla and mix just until blended. Do not mix the batter too much, or the cake will be tough. Stir in the pecans or walnuts by hand.

The batter will be very thick. Spoon it into the pan and spread evenly with the back of a spoon. Bake for 50 to 55 minutes, or until the top is brown and firm and a toothpick or cake tester inserted into the cake comes out clean.

Remove from the oven and cool on a rack for 10 minutes. Loosen the cake by sliding a knife around the perimeter between the cake and the

Mom Tip 2
Before you transfer the cake, to prevent the glaze from dripping onto the serving tray, cut four 3-inch-wide strips of wax paper and lay them on the edges of the empty tray. Then place the cake on top, so that each strip is partly under one edge. Crumbs and excess glaze will land on the wax paper, which can be pulled out and discarded once you've finished glazing the cake.

central metal tube. Place the rack on top of the cake and, with a pot holder on each hand, turn the cake pan and rack over together. If the cake doesn't slide out of the pan, tap it with the heel of your hand a few times. Let it finish cooling on the rack.

Transfer the cake to a serving plate (see Mom Tip 2). Spoon the glaze over the top and sides. Serve cold or at room temperature. Cover and refrigerate leftovers.

set aside to cool. The heat of the pot will melt the remaining chocolate.

Separate the eggs; discard 1 egg white. Put the whites in a large metal or ceramic bowl with no traces of grease. Set aside. Put the yolks in a food processor or a large bowl.

Add ¼ cup sugar to the yolks. Process, or beat with an electric mixer on high speed until pale yellow and frothy, about 2 minutes.

Beat the egg whites with an electric mixer just until they form stiff peaks. Do not overbeat. Gently beat in the remaining ¼ cup sugar, 2 tablespoons at a time, until all the sugar has been absorbed and the peaks have slightly softened, 1 to 2 minutes.

Add one-third of the egg whites to the yolk mixture and, using a rubber spatula, gently turn the mixture over on itself a few times to incorporate the whites. Add the rest of the egg whites and incorporate gently, turning the mixture over and over with the spatula until no streaks of white remain; the batter should remain fluffy.

Pour the batter into the pan and smooth the top. Bake for 15 to 18 minutes, or until the cake is firm and a toothpick or cake tester inserted into the cake comes out clean. Remove from the oven and set on a rack to cool. Loosen the cake by sliding a knife around the edges of the pan. The cake will fall slightly as it cools. After about 10 minutes, place a cooling rack over the top of the cake and, with a pot holder in each hand, carefully turn over the rack and cake pan. Remove the wax paper from the bottom of the cake. Cool to room temperature while upside down. Don't be concerned if the cake looks more like a thick pancake than a cake. Set aside.

Mom Tip 2
To remove the raspberry seeds, place a strainer over a small bowl. Pour the blended raspberries into the strainer and press them through the mesh with a spoon. Discard the seeds.

TO MAKE THE RASPBERRY GANACHE: Melt the chocolate in a heavy frying pan over very low heat, stirring constantly. When the chocolate has melted, add the cream and honey, and stir until the mixture is thick and glossy. Turn off the heat and set aside to cool.

Rinse the raspberries, and pat dry with a paper towel. Put in a food processor or blender and process for a few seconds, or until soupy (see Mom Tip 2). Transfer to a small pot, and cook over high heat for about 1 minute, or until hot. Add the butter and stir until it melts. Add the raspberry mixture to the chocolate mixture, and stir until combined. Set aside.

Pour ½ cup of the raspberry ganache into the bottom of the pie crust and spread it evenly to the sides. Place the cake on top. Pour the rest of the ganache around the sides and over the top of the cake. Cover and refrigerate for at least 45 minutes, or until needed.

Rinse the fresh raspberries, and pat dry with a paper towel. Decorate the tart with the raspberries, and serve.

Cherry-Chocolate Truffle Pie

Serves: 8–10 ⏱ Preparation time: 20 minutes + 20–110 minutes to make the crust ✎ Special equipment: Food processor or blender ✋ Chilling time: 3 hours ✍ Rating: Easy

Mom Tip 1
Fresh cherries are usually available for just a short time during the summer. Any sweet eating cherries, such as Bing, Lambert or Royal Ann, are suitable. Do not use sour cooking cherries. Thawed frozen cherries or drained canned cherries can also be used.

It was December when I first got this recipe, so I used frozen cherries. It was pretty good, but nowhere near as good as it is with fresh cherries. You may not want to hold off until summer to make it, but you should wait three hours for it to chill.

2 cups (about ½ pound) fresh sweet cherries (see Mom Tip 1)
½ cup sugar
8 squares (8 ounces) semisweet chocolate
¾ cup heavy cream
¼ teaspoon cherry extract or 2 tablespoons cherry liqueur
(see Mom Tip 2, page 216)

Mom Tip 2
Cherry extract is found near the vanilla extract in supermarkets or grocery stores. Cherry liqueurs, such as kirsch, are available in liquor stores.

Mom Tip 3
To intensify the cherry flavor, remove the pits from 1 more cup of cherries, and mix the extra cherries into the chocolate mixture along with the cherry sauce.

1 baked pie crust (see Mom Tip 2, page 139)
Whipped cream (page 275; optional)

Wash the cherries, pat them dry with paper towels and remove the pits. Set aside half to use as a topping. Combine the other half with the sugar in a food processor or blender and process until pureed. Set aside.

Melt the chocolate in a heavy frying pan over very low heat, stirring constantly. When the chocolate is almost melted, add the cream and keep stirring until the chocolate has melted and the cream has been incorporated. The mixture will be smooth and glossy. Turn off the heat and set aside to cool.

Stir in the cherry sauce (see Mom Tip 3) and the cherry extract or cherry liqueur. Pour the filling into the pie crust and chill for at least 3 hours or overnight. Decorate the top of the pie with the remaining cherries, and serve with whipped cream, if you like. Cover and refrigerate leftovers.

1953 Sir Edmund Hillary brings along chocolate for energy as he becomes the first man to climb Mount Everest. It's amazing how far some people will go to be alone with their chocolate.

Chocolate Strawberry Pie

Serves: 8–10 ⏱ Preparation time: 25 minutes + 20 minutes to make the crust ✎ Special equipment: Food processor or blender ✋ Chilling time: 3 hours ✌ Rating: Easy

When my wife, Jody, was pregnant, my mom held a baby shower for her. Jody insisted that I come along. It was twenty-five women and me. After an hour of opening presents, with Jody exclaiming "How cute!" every thirty seconds, we ate this pie. That day, I decided that I didn't want a large family after all, but I did discover a good dessert.

    1 cup (6-ounce package) semisweet chocolate chips
  ¼ cup heavy cream
    1 teaspoon vanilla extract
    1 baked Chocolate Crumb Crust (page 155)

If you buy strawberries in a box or basket, the berries occasionally have soft spots or, worse, white mold. Avoid less than perfect strawberries. Try to use strawberries the day you buy them, but if you must keep them overnight, store them in the refrigerator.

4 cups fresh ripe strawberries (see Mom Tip)
⅓ cup sugar
2½ tablespoons cornstarch
1 tablespoon lemon juice
  Whipped Cream (page 275; optional)

Melt the chocolate in a heavy frying pan over very low heat, stirring constantly. When the chocolate is almost melted, turn off the heat and set aside to cool. The heat of the pot will melt the remaining chocolate.

Stir in the cream, and mix thoroughly. If the chocolate separates into flecks, resume heating over very low heat for about 30 seconds, or until the chocolate blends into the cream. Remove from the heat, stir in the vanilla and cool for 5 minutes. Pour the mixture into the pie crust and spread it evenly. Set aside.

Remove the stems from the strawberries. Pat half of them dry with paper towels. Set aside. Combine the remaining strawberries, sugar, cornstarch and lemon juice in a food processor or blender and process for a few seconds, or until soupy.

Pour the strawberry mixture into a medium pot and cook over low heat, stirring constantly, for about 10 minutes, or until it comes to a boil and thickens. Pour the mixture over the chocolate layer in the pie crust. Cut the remaining strawberries in half and arrange them, cut side down, on top. Cover and refrigerate for at least 3 hours. Serve cold, with whipped cream, if you like. Cover and refrigerate leftovers.

Mid-1960s Carob becomes popular. Made from an evergreen shrub native to the Mediterranean region instead of the tropical cacao plant, carob is prepared in much the same way as chocolate. It's a worthy experiment, not unlike the attempts of medieval alchemists to make gold out of a cheese sandwich. However, the taste of this so-called chocolate substitute falls far short. Carob pods are also fed to livestock, a much more suitable use.

Chocolate Pizza

Serves: 10–12 ⓧ Preparation time: 20 minutes + 10–15 minutes for the icing or the Hot Fudge Sauce
🔥 Baking time: 15–20 minutes ✋ Cooling time: 20 minutes + 1 hour if using ice cream topping
🔪 Special equipment: 12-inch pizza pan (see Mom Tip) 🍴 Rating: Not So Easy

When my mom first mentioned the concept of this dessert, I imagined a regular pizza with a topping of chocolate chips mixed with pepperoni and anchovies. Thankfully, it's not that way at all. The whole crust is a big, round brownie, topped with chocolate sauce, coconut and chocolate chips. It looks really cool. This is one pizza where I won't leave all the crust ends sitting in the box.

CRUST

½ cup (1 stick) unsalted butter + more for greasing
3 ounces (3 squares) unsweetened chocolate
1¼ cups sugar
2 large eggs

1 teaspoon vanilla extract
½ cup all-purpose flour
¼ teaspoon baking powder
¼ teaspoon salt

"Sauce"

1 pint ice cream or ½ cup icing (Chocolate Buttercream
Icing, page 68, Couldn't-Be-Simpler Chocolate Icing,
page 65, or Ganache, page 70)

Choose 2 or 3 toppings from the following

½ cup semisweet, milk or white chocolate chips
¼ cup peanut butter chips
¼ cup sweetened shredded coconut
½ cup chopped nuts
1 cup sliced fresh strawberries, kiwis or bananas
½ cup fresh raspberries, blackberries or blueberries
¼ cup Candied Orange Peel (page 21)
10–12 maraschino cherries
½ cup Hot Fudge Sauce to drizzle on top of everything, if
using ice cream (page 238)

Kids' Toppings

1 cup M&M's or other little candies
1 cup mini marshmallows
½ cup chocolate sprinkles

☞ Mom Tip
Pizza pans are available at some grocery stores and specialty cookware shops. You can substitute a 9-x-13-inch cake pan if you don't mind serving square or rectangular slices of pizza.

To make the crust: Place an oven rack in the middle position and preheat the oven to 350°. Cover a 12-inch pizza pan with aluminum foil (see Mom Tip). Lightly rub the foil with butter. Set aside.

Melt the chocolate and butter in a small, heavy pot over very low heat, stirring occasionally. When the chocolate is almost melted, turn off the heat and set aside to cool. The heat of the pot will melt the remaining chocolate.

Put the sugar, eggs and vanilla in a food processor or a large bowl. Process, or beat with an electric mixer for about 2 minutes on high speed, until pale yellow and frothy. Add the chocolate mixture, and process or beat until well blended. Add the flour, baking powder and salt, and pulse for about 10 seconds or beat on low speed just until blended.

Pour the batter into the foil-lined pizza pan, and spread evenly with the back of a spoon. Bake for 15 to 20 minutes, or until the crust is firm to the touch. Remove from the oven and cool on a rack for 3 minutes. Carefully lift the foil and pizza crust from the pan and let the crust cool directly on the rack. It will cool much faster out of the pan.

To make the "sauce": If you are using ice cream, remove it from the freezer to begin softening, or soften by microwaving it (in its container) at low/medium speed for about 30 seconds. If you are using icing, make it now.

When the crust is at room temperature, carefully lift the foil and crust off the rack. Place the rack on top of the crust and very carefully turn the crust and rack over together. Gently pull the foil away from the bottom of the crust, making sure not to crack or break it. Place a tray face down on the crust and, holding it firmly, turn the rack, crust and tray

☀! Mom Warning
Do not freeze fresh
fruit. It will become
mushy when it thaws.

over together. Remove the rack. The crust is now ready for the sauce and toppings.

TO TOP THE PIZZA: Spread it with a ½-inch layer of ice cream or a thin layer of icing. Decorate with 2 or 3 of the toppings or put them in small bowls and let guests select their own. Do not add the fresh fruit to the pizza until you are about to serve it (see Mom Warning).

If your pizza is topped with ice cream, put it in the freezer for 1 hour to firm up before serving. If it is topped with icing, you can serve it immediately or leave it at room temperature for a few hours until needed. Cut the pizza into 10 or 12 slices and serve. Cover and freeze ice cream–topped leftovers; cover and refrigerate icing-topped leftovers.

1964 Roald Dahl's children's book <u>Charlie and the Chocolate Factory</u> is published. It's the story of a small boy named Charlie who, through simple virtue and a pure love of chocolate, inherits Willy Wonka's magnificent candy company. It's also a harrowing tale of an oppressed work-force, known as the Oompa Loompas, who are paid only in chocolate and are never allowed to see the sun. One day the Oompa Loompas will unionize and demand better pay and an on-site day care center. But until then, it's Everlasting Gobstoppers for everyone.

Minty Ice Cream Sandwiches

Makes: 8–10 sandwiches Preparation time: 30 minutes Baking time: 14–16 minutes (7–8 minutes per batch) if using cookie sheets; 10 minutes if using muffin pans Chilling time: About 1 hour Rating: Not So Easy

Ice cream sandwiches taught me that the world was a harsh place. When I was in fourth grade, a big kid named Chris proposed that if I gave him fifty cents so he could get an ice cream sandwich, he would give me two dollars the next day. I couldn't believe my good fortune. But when I went up to Chris the next day and asked him for the money, he told me he didn't remember and that it was in my best interest to forget as well. I think Chris works on Wall Street now.

But don't worry about me. I've discovered a way to make ice cream sandwiches without having to leave the house. They're not as symmetrical as the ones that come out of a box, but it's not the shape that matters — it's what's stuffed in the middle.

1 pint ice cream, any flavor
½ cup (1 stick) unsalted butter + more for greasing
4 squares (4 ounces) semisweet chocolate
1 square (1 ounce) unsweetened chocolate
⅔ cup brown sugar
1 large egg
1 teaspoon peppermint extract
1 cup all-purpose flour
½ teaspoon baking powder
¼ teaspoon salt

Remove the ice cream from the freezer to begin softening, or microwave it (in its container) at low/medium for about 30 seconds.

Place an oven rack in the middle position and preheat the oven to 375°. Lightly rub two cookie sheets or two 12-cup muffin pans with butter, or use nonstick baking sheets or muffin pans. Set aside.

Melt both the chocolates and butter in a heavy frying pan over very low heat, stirring occasionally. When the chocolate is almost melted, turn off the heat and set aside to cool. The heat of the pan will melt the remaining chocolate.

Put the brown sugar, egg and peppermint extract in a food processor or a large bowl. Process, or beat with an electric mixer until smooth and creamy. Add the cooled chocolate mixture, and process or beat until well blended. Add the flour, baking powder and salt, and process or beat on low speed just until blended.

IF USING COOKIE SHEETS: To make 16 cookies for 8 large sandwiches, scoop 2 teaspoons of dough, and shape into 2-inch rounds. For slightly smaller sandwiches (20 cookies), scoop 1½ teaspoons of dough, and shape into 2-inch rounds. Flatten them with your hands to about ¼-inch thickness, and place on the cookie sheets, leaving at least ½ inch of space between each cookie. Bake each batch, one cookie sheet at a time, for 7 to 8 minutes, or until the cookies feel firm to the touch. Remove from the oven, and cool on the sheet for about 3 minutes. Then transfer them with a spatula to a cooling rack.

IF USING MUFFIN PANS: Spoon 1 heaping teaspoon of dough into 20 muffin spaces and flatten them with the back of the spoon. Bake for about 10 minutes. Remove from the oven, and cool in the muffin pans for about 3 minutes. Then transfer them to a cooling rack.

When the cookies are cool, spoon 1 or 2 tablespoons softened ice cream onto the flat side of one cookie (see Mom Warning). Gently place a second cookie, flat side against the ice cream, on top. Wrap each cookie in foil or plastic wrap, and return to the freezer until firm, or for at least 1 hour. Serve frozen.

Chocolate Profiteroles

Serves: 4 (4–5 profiteroles per person) Preparation time: 15 minutes Baking time: 25–30 minutes Rating: Easy

Profiteroles are ice cream sandwiches for people who took a little French in high school.

¼ cup (½ stick) unsalted butter + more for greasing
½ cup water
1 teaspoon sugar
¼ teaspoon salt
½ cup all-purpose flour
1 tablespoon unsweetened cocoa powder
2 large eggs
 Ice cream or Ganache (page 70)

※✕! Mom Warning
If the dough is too hot
to touch, wait for at
least 1 minute before
adding the first egg,
because if you add
raw egg to the dough
when it's too hot, the
egg will cook rather
than blend into the
dough. But if the
dough is too cold, it
won't blend in easily.

𝒞 Mom Tip
Another way to make
these puffs is to trans-
fer the warm dough to
a small plastic storage
bag, cut off one of the
corners and squeeze
the dough onto the
baking sheet in small
mounds.

Place an oven rack in the middle position and preheat the oven to 400°. Lightly rub a cookie sheet with butter, or use a nonstick baking sheet. Set aside.

Put the water, butter, sugar and salt in a medium pot and place over high heat. When the mixture comes to a boil, add the flour and cocoa. Stir quickly with a wooden spoon until it forms a ball. Remove from the heat, and turn the ball of dough over a few times. Cool in the pan for about 5 minutes (see Mom Warning). Add the eggs to the dough, one at a time, beating thoroughly each time until the egg has been well incorporated. When the dough becomes shiny and soft, it's ready for baking.

Spoon rounded teaspoons of the dough onto the cookie sheet (see Mom Tip), leaving 1 inch between each piece. There will be 16 to 22 little puffs.

Bake for 25 to 30 minutes, or until the pastry has puffed and is firm to the touch. Remove from the oven, and immediately transfer with a spatula to a cooling rack. Cool to room temperature.

If serving with ice cream, remove the ice cream from the freezer to begin softening, or microwave it (in its container) at low/medium for about 30 seconds. Or make Ganache.

To assemble the profiteroles, cut each puff in half. Using a spoon, scrape out any mushy dough in either half and discard it. Spoon some softened ice cream or ganache into the bottom half. Place the other half on top. Place 4 or 5 profiteroles on each dessert plate. Serve immediately.

Mississippi Mud Pie

Serves: 8–10 ⏱ Preparation time: 20 minutes + 20 minutes for the crust and 10 minutes for the Hot Fudge Sauce ✋ Chilling time: 2 hours ✌ Rating: Easy

Mom Tip 1
If you like a lot of ice cream in your pie, you can use up to ½ gallon. It's surprising how much ice cream a pie crust can hold.

Mom Tip 2
If you don't have time to make your own pie crust, a store-bought chocolate crumb crust will work, although it's not as good.

My earliest gourmet efforts were the mud pies my sister and I would make in the yard after it rained. We'd add a few candles and try to convince my dad to eat them. He'd get one about two inches away from his mouth before he'd start laughing. Perhaps it was the grass and twigs that gave us away.

The adult version of mud pie is far more tempting. You can use whatever kind of ice cream suits your taste.

  1 quart chocolate or coffee ice cream (see Mom Tip 1)
 ¼ cup slivered or sliced almonds
1¼ cups Hot Fudge Sauce (page 238)
  1 baked and cooled Chocolate Crumb Crust (page 155;
    see Mom Tip 2)

Remove the ice cream from the freezer to begin softening, or microwave it (in its container) at low/medium for about 30 seconds.

Place an oven rack in the middle position and preheat the oven to 350°. Spread the almonds on a cookie sheet and bake them for about 5 minutes, or until they begin to turn golden brown. Be careful they don't burn. Remove from the oven and set aside to cool.

Make the hot fudge sauce. Cool to lukewarm. Spoon ½ cup into the bottom of the pie crust, smoothing it evenly with the back of the spoon. Set the rest of the sauce aside. Fill the pie crust with the softened ice cream, and smooth the top as much as possible. Place it in the freezer for about 1 hour, or until the ice cream has hardened.

Remove from the freezer and spoon the rest of the sauce over the top, covering as much of the pie as possible. The sauce will harden, so work quickly. Sprinkle the almonds on top, and press them into the chocolate so they don't fall off. Return the pie to the freezer for about 1 hour, or until the sauce is frozen. If you're not serving the pie right away, put it inside a large self-sealing plastic freezer bag and store in the freezer until needed, but no longer than 1 week. If you remove this pie from the freezer about 30 minutes before you plan to serve it, it will be easier to cut.

Sauces

Does this ever happen to you? You're in a chocolate-craving mood, and all you have in the house is vanilla ice cream. You don't know how it got there, but there it is. You know it won't be a good substitute for chocolate, but it will calm you down and fill your stomach. The dilemma disappears if you can make your own chocolate sauce. You can finish a whole quart of vanilla if you add a little Hot Fudge Sauce. And if you happen to make a mistake while preparing a dessert, you can hide its flaws with Chocolate Syrup. Chocolate sauces are like a baking first-aid kit.

Bittersweet Dessert Sauce ★ 232
Chocolate-Mocha Sauce ★ 234

Chocolate Syrup ★ 236
Hot Fudge Sauce ★ 238

1969–1973 Chocolate is eaten on the moon. While the inhabitants of Earth try to get the ringing out of their ears from Woodstock, 240,000 miles away, the Apollo astronauts enjoy cocoa on the Sea of Tranquillity. The chocolate provides a welcome burst of flavor after a meal of freeze-dried lima beans.

Bittersweet Dessert Sauce

Makes: About 1 cup Preparation time: 10 minutes Rating: Very Easy

This sauce has no milk or cream in it, which makes for a more intense chocolate kick than regular chocolate sauce.

Mom Tip
Using high-quality chocolate, such as Hawaiian Vintage, Scharffen Berger or Valrhona, can make a difference in flavor here.

4 squares (4 ounces) bittersweet chocolate (see Mom Tip)
2 tablespoons unsalted butter
⅓ cup water
½ teaspoon vanilla extract, peppermint extract (for mint flavor) or Kahlúa (for coffee flavor)

Combine the chocolate, butter and water in a heavy frying pan and heat over low heat, stirring occasionally. Bring the mixture to a boil and cook for 1 minute, stirring constantly. Remove from the heat and stir in the vanilla, peppermint or Kahlúa. Serve immediately, or let cool and then serve.

Refrigerate leftovers in a glass or plastic jar or a small, self-sealing plastic bag. To return to room temperature, place the container in a bowl of hot water or reheat in the microwave.

1980s Chocolate gets an image makeover. As Americans turn their attention to solving the Rubik's Cube, chocolate reverses its decade-long slide. The truffle captures the heart of the country, and soon chocolate-lovers are paying up to $20 a pound for premium chocolate. Business lesson: How do you get a product out of the doldrums? Quadruple the price.

Chocolate-Mocha Sauce

Makes: About 1 cup   Preparation time: 15 minutes   Rating: Very Easy

To me, nothing smells better and tastes worse than coffee. But when it's combined with chocolate, it finally tastes as good as it smells. This chocolate sauce, which has coffee as a key ingredient, will make you give up your squeeze bottle of chocolate sauce for good.

Mom Tip
If you don't have half-and-half (half cream and half milk), substitute milk, which will make the sauce slightly thinner, or heavy cream, which will make the sauce slightly thicker.

- ⅓ cup unsweetened cocoa powder
- ⅓ cup sugar
- 1 teaspoon instant coffee granules
- ½ cup half-and-half (see Mom Tip)
- ¼ cup light corn syrup
- ¼ cup semisweet chocolate chips
- 1 tablespoon unsalted butter
- 1 teaspoon vanilla extract

Combine the cocoa, sugar, coffee granules, half-and-half and corn syrup in a small, heavy pot, and stir until combined. Bring the mixture to a boil over medium heat, stirring occasionally. Remove from the heat and add the chocolate chips. Stir occasionally for about 1 minute, or until the chips have melted. Add the butter and vanilla and stir until the butter has melted. Serve immediately, or let cool and serve.

Refrigerate leftovers in a glass or plastic jar or a small, self-sealing plastic bag. To return to room temperature, place the container in a bowl of hot water or reheat in the microwave.

Chocolate Syrup

Makes: 1 cup 🕙 Preparation time: 5 minutes 🔥 Cooking time: 5 minutes ✍ Rating: Very Easy

I never got to meet my maternal grandfather, but my mom told me that he liked to drink chocolate syrup right from the can. Once I heard that, I felt as though I knew him. I don't tend to drink it myself, but chocolate syrup does make almost everything taste better. And when you make it at home, you can leave out the potassium sorbate.

Mom Tip
If you're serving this with Chocolate Waffles (page 22), use maple syrup instead of the light corn syrup.

½ cup unsweetened cocoa powder
½ cup brown sugar
½ cup water
⅓ cup light corn syrup (see Mom Tip)
1 teaspoon vanilla extract

Put the cocoa, brown sugar, water and corn syrup in a small pot and bring to a boil over high heat, stirring continually. Cook for 1 minute. Remove from the heat and let cool. Stir in the vanilla. Serve immediately, or when needed.

Refrigerate leftovers in a glass or plastic jar or a small, self-sealing plastic bag. To return to room temperature, place the container in a bowl of hot water, or reheat in the microwave.

Hot Fudge Sauce

Makes: About 1½ cups ⏱ Preparation time: 10 minutes ♨ Rating: Very Easy

To me, the greatest invention of the last one hundred years is hot fudge sauce. It's sad that so many generations didn't get to taste it. If Shakespeare had tried it, maybe he would have been in a better mood when he wrote *Romeo and Juliet*, and the two star-crossed lovers would have ended up running off to get hitched in Vegas.

⅔ cup brown sugar
½ cup unsweetened cocoa powder
½ cup heavy cream
2 tablespoons unsalted butter
¼ teaspoon salt

Combine all the ingredients in a small, heavy pot and stir thoroughly. Bring to a boil over medium heat, stirring constantly. Cook for 1 minute more, continuing to stir, until smooth. Remove from the heat. Serve immediately, or let cool and serve.

Refrigerate leftovers in a glass or plastic jar or a small, self-sealing plastic bag. To return to room temperature, place the container in a bowl of hot water or reheat in the microwave.

Candy

Candy seems like a magical food that can only be made in top-secret candy company laboratories. But that's not true. You may not be able to duplicate the formula for a Hershey Bar, but it turns out you can make mighty good truffles and fudge in your own kitchen. Plus, when you make your own candy, you can avoid having to engage in a life-and-death struggle with that vending machine.

Chocolate-Covered Nuts and Other Goodies ★ 242

Surprisingly Easy Fudge ★ 244

Orange Fudge ★ 246

Chocolate Almond Crunch ★ 248

Peanut Butter and Chocolate Chunks ★ 250

Truffles ★ 252

1990 Mars products are introduced in Moscow. It's the end of the Cold War, and the Russians open the drapes to see what they've missed in the last seventy years. They're not sure what to make of hula hoops or The Partridge Family, but there's no doubt in their minds about candy bars. The line at the first Mars outlet extends for a quarter of a mile, which must have seemed like the express lane after decades of bread lines.

Chocolate-Covered Nuts and Other Goodies

Makes: 24 pieces · Preparation time: 15 minutes · Chilling time: 30 minutes · Rating: Very Easy

When my mom has leftover melted chocolate, she'll find a use for it. Psychologically incapable of throwing it away, she'll dip nuts, pretzels, marshmallows, even crystallized ginger. My favorite is marshmallows. These remind me of Mallomars.

6 squares (6 ounces) semisweet or bittersweet chocolate

1 CUP OF ANY OF THE FOLLOWING

Hazelnuts
Peanuts
Miniature marshmallows
Raisins
Candied Orange Peel (page 21)
Crystallized ginger

Melt the chocolate in a heavy frying pan over very low heat, stirring constantly. When the chocolate is almost melted, turn off the heat and set aside to cool. The heat of the pan will melt the remaining chocolate.

Place a large sheet of wax paper on a cookie sheet and set aside. Add the cup of nuts or other ingredient of choice to the melted chocolate and stir gently until everything is covered with chocolate (see Mom Tip). Scoop up 1 teaspoon of the chocolate mixture and place on the wax paper. Continue until all the chocolate mixture is gone.

Refrigerate the candy for 30 minutes, or until the chocolate has completely hardened. Store at room temperature in a closed container or wrapped in foil or plastic.

Surprisingly Easy Fudge

Makes: 36 pieces ⏲ Preparation time: 15 minutes ✋ Cooling time: 1 hour ♨ Rating: Very Easy

How can it be? How can you make fudge out of only two ingredients (or three, if you're one of those people who likes to mix it with nuts)? Using ice cream is a great shortcut, because it replaces both milk and butter, as well as adding more chocolate. It tastes just as good as a more traditional (and difficult) fudge.

Mom Tip 1
Any ice cream flavor will do. It will change the flavor of the fudge only slightly.

Butter for greasing
16 squares (16 ounces) bittersweet or semisweet chocolate
1 cup chocolate ice cream (see Mom Tip 1)
½ cup chopped walnuts (optional)

Line an 8- or 9-inch square pan with aluminum foil, making sure that two ends of the foil overhang the pan by about 2 inches so you can easily lift the fudge out of the pan later. Lightly rub the bottom and sides of the foil with butter. Set aside.

☞ Mom Tip 2
To make the fudge more chunky, add ½ cup miniature marsh-mallows, peanut but-ter chips or white chocolate chips when you add the walnuts.

Melt the chocolate in a heavy frying pan over very low heat, stirring constantly. When the chocolate is almost melted, turn off the heat and set aside to cool. The heat of the pan will melt the remaining chocolate. Stir in the ice cream. When it has melted, add the nuts, if using, and stir until combined (see Mom Tip 2). Pour the fudge into the prepared pan, smoothing it into the corners with the back of a spoon. Refrigerate until firm, about 1 hour.

Carefully lift the ends of the foil and remove the fudge from the pan. Peel off and discard the foil. Place the fudge on a cutting board and, using a large knife, cut it into 36 pieces. Store at room temperature in a closed container or wrapped in foil or plastic.

Orange Fudge

Makes: 36 pieces 🕐 Preparation time: 20 minutes ✋ Cooling time: 1 hour 🍴 Rating: Easy

This is how fudge should taste. I know it's a little odd, what with melting marshmallows and shaving a perfectly good orange, but it all adds up.

🖐 Mom Tip 1
Evaporated milk, which is milk with some of the water removed, is stocked near the powdered milk in the supermarket. Don't confuse it with sweetened condensed milk, also available in small cans, which is thicker and sweeter.

½ cup (1 stick) unsalted butter + more for greasing
2 cups sugar
1 can (5 ounces) evaporated milk (see Mom Tip 1)
10 large marshmallows or 1 cup miniature marshmallows
1 cup (6-ounce package) semisweet chocolate chips
1 tablespoon grated peel from 1 small orange
½ teaspoon Cointreau or other orange liqueur
 (see Mom Tip 2)
1 cup chopped walnuts (optional)

Line an 8- or 9-inch square baking pan with aluminum foil, making sure that two ends of the foil overhang the pan by about 2 inches so you can easily lift the fudge out of the pan later. Lightly rub the bottom and sides of the foil with butter. Set aside.

Combine the sugar, evaporated milk and marshmallows in a medium pot and begin heating over medium-high heat, stirring constantly. When it comes to a boil, turn down the heat to medium, set a timer for 6 minutes and continue stirring. The marshmallows will eventually melt, and the mixture will become very foamy.

Remove the pot from the heat and stir in the chocolate chips, butter, orange peel, orange liqueur and the walnuts, if using. Stir vigorously for 2 or 3 minutes, or until the fudge is smooth and creamy. Pour the fudge into the prepared pan, smoothing it into the corners with the back of a spoon. Refrigerate until firm, about 1 hour.

Carefully lift the ends of the foil and remove the fudge from the pan. Peel off and discard the foil. Place the fudge on a cutting board and, using a large knife, cut it into 36 pieces. Store at room temperature in a closed container or wrapped in foil or plastic.

Chocolate Almond Crunch

Makes: 24–36 pieces ⏲ Preparation time: 20 minutes ✋ Cooling time: 10 minutes ❧ Special equipment: Candy thermometer (see Mom Tip 1) ☙ Rating: Easy

~~~~~~

C hocolate Almond Crunch has the consistency of peanut brittle but tastes like chocolate. It's perfect if you like your chocolate candy to bite you back instead of slowly melting away.

Mom Tip 1
Candy thermometers are available in kitchen gadget and department stores. They cost anywhere from $8 to $15. Choose one with a large, easy-to-read dial.

½ cup (1 stick) unsalted butter + more for greasing
2 tablespoons milk
1 tablespoon corn syrup
¾ cup sugar
3 tablespoons unsweetened cocoa powder
½ cup slivered or sliced almonds

Line a cookie sheet with aluminum foil and wipe the foil with a bit of butter. Set aside.

Combine the butter, milk and corn syrup in a medium, heavy pot (see

🖙 Mom Tip 2
The heavier and thicker-bottomed the pot is, the less likely you are to burn the candy.

Mom Tip 2) and begin heating over medium-high heat. When the butter has melted and the mixture becomes frothy, add the sugar. Stir until combined. Attach a candy thermometer to the side of the pot and cook without stirring until the mixtures reaches 222°. The mixture will be bubbling steadily and will have changed from white to golden tan, 5 to 7 minutes. Turn off the heat and add the cocoa. Stir quickly until it dissolves. Add the almonds and stir to incorporate.

Quickly pour the chocolate mixture onto the foil and, with a knife or metal spatula, spread it thinly to about ¼-inch thickness. Don't worry if some parts are thicker than others. Let cool for 10 minutes, or until it reaches room temperature. Peel off the foil and discard. Cut or break the candy into pieces. Store at room temperature in a closed container or wrapped in foil or plastic.

1996 The journal Nature reports that chemicals found in chocolate affect the same brain receptor system targeted by marijuana. But a 130-pound person would have to eat 25 pounds of chocolate in one sitting to get a noticeable buzz. A worthy challenge indeed.

Peanut Butter and Chocolate Chunks

Makes: 25 (1½-inch) squares Preparation time: 15 minutes Chilling time: 15 minutes
Rating: Very Easy

My brother-in-law Tom has always laughed at our family's devotion to chocolate. But when my mom made these, he came back for seconds and thirds, saying, "They're worth getting a stomachache."

Mom Tip
I prefer crunchy peanut butter cups, so I use chunky peanut butter. If you like the more traditional peanut butter cups, use creamy peanut butter.

- 2 tablespoons unsalted butter, softened to room temperature, + more for greasing
- 4 squares (4 ounces) semisweet chocolate
- 1¼ cups powdered sugar
- ¾ cup peanut butter (see Mom Tip)
- ¼ cup brown sugar
- 1 teaspoon milk + more if needed
- ¼ teaspoon salt

Line an 8- or 9-inch square pan with aluminum foil, making sure that the ends of the foil overhang the pan by about 2 inches so you can easily lift the candy out of the pan later. Lightly rub the bottom and sides of the foil with butter. Set aside.

Melt the chocolate in a small, heavy pot over very low heat, stirring constantly. When the chocolate is almost melted, turn off the heat and set aside to cool. The heat of the pot will melt the remaining chocolate.

Put the remaining ingredients in a food processor or a large bowl. Process, or beat with an electric mixer until smooth and creamy. Taste to see if the mixture is too dry and crumbly. If you want it smoother and creamier, add another teaspoon or more of milk and mix until it reaches the consistency you prefer. It should remain firm enough to pick up without sticking to your fingers.

Transfer the mixture to the foil-lined pan, and press into a flat, even layer with the back of a large spoon. Spread the melted chocolate in a thin layer over the top of the peanut butter mixture. Refrigerate uncovered for 15 minutes to let the chocolate harden.

Carefully lift the ends of the foil and remove the candy from the pan. Cut into 25 squares and serve. Store in a closed container or wrapped in foil or plastic.

1997 Europe separates into two chocolate factions. One group, led by Belgium and France, objects to the chocolate policies of the other group, led by Britain and Denmark. The Belgians and French claim the British and Danes allow companies to substitute vegetable fats for cocoa butter, a practice that threatens the chocolate's purity. They also claim that the British and the Danes use too much milk in their milk chocolate. This situation should be closely monitored by NATO. World War I started over less than this.

Truffles

Makes: 15–18 (1-inch) truffles 🕒 Preparation time: 30 minutes 🤚 Cooling time: 2 hours 🍫 Rating: Easy

If you make truffles at home, you don't have to set aside a paycheck to finance a few dozen. They may not be as pretty as the ones you have to stand in line for, and they don't come in a fancy box—unless you put them in one yourself—but they do taste awfully good.

🖎 Mom Tip 1
This is a case where using the finest chocolate, such as Hawaiian Vintage, Scharffen Berger or Valrhona, can make a difference.

6 squares (6 ounces) semisweet or bittersweet chocolate (see Mom Tip 1)
⅓ cup heavy cream
2 teaspoons unsalted butter
1–2 teaspoons liqueur (see Mom Tip 2) or 1 teaspoon vanilla extract
¼ cup unsweetened cocoa powder or powdered sugar or sweetened cocoa (see Mom Tip 3) + more if needed

Melt the chocolate in a heavy frying pan over very low heat, stirring constantly. When the chocolate is almost melted, turn off the heat and set aside to cool. The heat of the pan will melt the remaining chocolate.

Add the cream and butter and stir until the butter has melted. Add the liqueur or vanilla and stir for 1 minute, or until the mixture is thick and glossy. Transfer to a bowl and refrigerate, uncovered, for about 1½ hours, or until firm.

Put the cocoa or powdered sugar in a small bowl. Set aside. Set out a small sieve and a plate for the finished truffles.

Remove the truffle mixture from the refrigerator. Scrape a teaspoon across the top to make a ball about 1 inch across. If you like small truffles, make the balls ¾ inch or ½ inch across. The chocolate mixture is stiff, so the balls will not be perfectly round. Use the spoon to shape them. Do not shape them with your hands, because the chocolate will start to melt.

Gently place the ball in the cocoa or powdered sugar, and roll it around until it is covered. Using a spoon, place the truffle in the sieve and shake it vigorously over the sink or a large plate. The shaking will remove any excess cocoa or sugar, and it will also help make the truffle more round. With the spoon, transfer the completed truffle to the serving plate. Repeat the process until all the truffles have been formed, adding more cocoa or powdered sugar as needed. Don't let the truffles touch each other on the plate. If the plate isn't big enough, either use a second plate or place a sheet of wax paper over the completed truffles and place another layer on top.

Store, covered, in the refrigerator for at least 30 minutes before serving. Truffles will keep for about a week—in case something large falls on you and prevents you from getting to the fridge.

☞ Mom Tip 2
Flavored liqueurs will give the truffles a subtle flavor. Try Kahlúa (coffee), Cointreau (orange), Crème de Fraises (raspberry) or cognac, Grand Marnier or rum. If you want just a hint of flavor, use 1 teaspoon liqueur. If you want a stronger flavor, use 1 tablespoon.

☞ Mom Tip 3
Unsweetened cocoa has a bitter flavor and may not be to everyone's taste. Powdered sugar or sweetened cocoa adds a touch of sweetness.

Drinks

C hocolate drinks have changed a lot since the early days. Having Mexican Hot Chocolate is a good way to bond with centuries of chocolate drinkers. It's comforting to know that you're part of a long tradition of chocolate gluttony.

Parisian Hot Chocolate ★ 256   Untraditional Chocolate Soda ★ 260
Mexican Hot Chocolate ★ 258

1997 The <u>New York Times</u> reports that cacao trees are in trouble, under siege from fungal and viral diseases and insects. In five to ten years, the world will experience a shortage of cocoa. Holy cellulite! It's time to mobilize! Get Sting out there with a microphone! Whales and spotted owls are nice, but when the chocolate supplies are threatened, it's time to send Bruce Willis into the jungle.

Parisian Hot Chocolate

Serves: 4 ⓠ Preparation time: 15 minutes ⚖ Rating: Very Easy

When our family took a trip to Paris last year, I let others do the talking, but I did learn to ask for *chocolat chaud*. It was richer and creamier than I was used to, and it made me feel like one of the 1920s Lost Generation. But now that I'm back in mainstream suburban life, I can make my own version, and I don't have to worry about my accent.

Mom Tip
To make a very rich version of Parisian Hot Chocolate, substitute 1 cup heavy cream for 1 cup of the milk.

4 squares (4 ounces) semisweet chocolate
2½ cups milk (see Mom Tip)
1 tablespoon sugar
½ teaspoon vanilla extract
Whipped cream (page 275; optional)

Melt the chocolate in a small, heavy pot over very low heat, stirring constantly. When the chocolate is almost melted, turn off the heat and set aside to cool. The heat of the pot will melt the remaining chocolate.

Put the milk and sugar in a medium pot and place over medium-high heat, stirring occasionally. When the mixture begins to bubble around the edges, remove from the heat and stir in the melted chocolate. Add the vanilla, and stir until the mixture is fully blended.

Pour into cups and spoon on some whipped cream, if you like. Serve immediately.

1999 Mars and Hershey dominate the American candy bar market. Eighteen of the top twenty brands are owned by one of the two hulking chocolate masses. Hershey alone has more than 90 million cacao beans in its storage facility, enough for 55 billion candy bars. Your needs will be provided for.

Mexican Hot Chocolate

Serves: 4 ⏲ Preparation time: 15 minutes ✋ Rating: Very Easy

~~~~~~

When my sister Bonnie was a teenager, she rebelled by going to other countries. She spent one summer with a family in Mexico and wrote us letters about how she hated the food but loved a boy named Adrian. My parents tried to be happy for her. She also mentioned that she liked the hot chocolate down there, and when she returned, she brought back a five-pound bag of cocoa, a gift from Adrian. Occasionally, I would catch Bonnie wistfully caressing the bag. My parents were relieved when it was finally empty.

Bonnie begged Mom to keep making Mexican Hot Chocolate, so she developed a recipe that didn't rely on cocoa.

  2 squares (2 ounces) unsweetened chocolate
  ½ teaspoon ground cinnamon or 1 cinnamon stick
  2½ cups milk

2 tablespoons sugar + more if needed
½ teaspoon vanilla extract

Melt the chocolate in a small, heavy pot over very low heat, stirring constantly. When the chocolate is almost melted, stir in the ground cinnamon (if you are using the cinnamon stick, add it later), turn off the heat and set aside to cool. The heat of the pot will melt the remaining chocolate.

Put the milk and sugar in a medium pot and place over medium-high heat, stirring occasionally. If you are using a cinnamon stick, put it into the milk mixture as it is heating. When the mixture begins to bubble around the edges, remove from the heat and take out and discard the cinnamon stick.

Stir in the melted chocolate and vanilla. Then, using a whisk, beat until the mixture is foamy.

Pour into cups and serve immediately. Offer more sugar, so people can sweeten to their taste.

Untraditional Chocolate Soda

Serves: 4 ⏲ Preparation time: 5 minutes + 10 minutes for the Chocolate Syrup ✎ Special equipment: Blender ♨ Rating: Very Easy

When I was nine, and Mom was trying to convince me that moving to America from England would be fun, she would tell me that there were soda fountains on every corner and how she always insisted on having chocolate ice cream in her chocolate soda instead of the traditional vanilla. When we got here, it turned out that she was living in the past, and I was stuck drinking Slurpees from the mini-mart. Recently she tried to recapture the taste from her youth. I'll admit that these chocolate sodas are awfully good. I have twenty years of catching up to do.

> 2 cups chocolate ice cream
> 1⅓ cups seltzer water
> ¼ cup Chocolate Syrup (page 236)

Combine the ice cream, seltzer water and chocolate syrup in a blender and blend until smooth. Pour into glasses and serve.

Or, if you like to spoon your ice cream out of the glass, make individual sodas right in the glass. Combine ⅓ cup seltzer water and 1 tablespoon chocolate syrup in each of four tall glasses. Add ½ cup ice cream to each soda. Serve with straws and long spoons.

Questions Beginning Chocoholics Often Ask

~~~~~~

Should I be afraid of cooking with chocolate?

Only if you're the type of person who is normally frightened by food. Chocolate does require a small amount of patience and technique, but you don't have to study under a French master to get the hang of it. If you can fry an egg, you can cook with chocolate. However, if your idea of making a soufflé is throwing eggs into the oven and turning the heat up, perhaps you should order out.

What are the seven dangers of cooking with chocolate?

1. Don't melt chocolate over high heat. Anybody who's eaten a chocolate bar on a hot day knows how easily chocolate melts. If you rush the melting process, you'll burn the chocolate and turn it into an encrusted brown mess that won't come back to life.

2. Don't mix small amounts of liquid with melting chocolate. For some reason known only to university physicists and telephone psychics, you can melt large amounts of liquid with chocolate but not one to two drops. The small amount causes the chocolate to get stiff and grainy.

If you insist on making this mistake, as I have several times, you have three options. The first is to add more liquid and then stir. The result will be runnier than you'd like, but it may still be usable. The second is to add 1 to 2 tablespoons vegetable oil or solid vegetable shortening, such as Crisco — not butter or margarine, because they contain small amounts of water. The chocolate may or may not revert to a smooth, usable state. You will have to adjust the recipe to account for the extra fat you've added: if you added 1 tablespoon vegetable oil, subtract 1 tablespoon butter from the ingredients. The third option is to chuck it and start over.

3. Don't add hot melted chocolate to raw eggs or to an egg-butter mixture. The heat will start to cook the eggs or melt the butter, causing a chain reaction that may get a man killed — or at least change the texture of what you're making.

4. Beware of adding melted chocolate to any cold mixture. Particles of chocolate may solidify, interfering with the all-important texture.

5. Don't buy the wrong kind of chocolate. If you use semisweet chocolate instead of unsweetened chocolate, the result will be so sickly sweet that you'll only be able to eat half of it before admitting that it's too sweet even for you. Another common mistake is confusing unsweetened cocoa with the sweetened cocoa used for chocolate milk. Don't even think about doing that.

6. Don't buy artificial chocolate. You may save a little money, but artificial chocolate or a substitute such as carob will leave you feeling hollow inside.

7. Beware your oven's cooking temperature. I'm a trusting sort, so I tend to believe the dial on the front of my oven. But don't be fooled. Ovens can be as much as 100 degrees off, causing your dessert to come out too dry or too gooey. So buy an oven thermometer — they cost $10 or less — and test your oven before trusting it with your chocolate.

What are the different kinds of chocolate and how do I know which ones to use?

Follow the recipes. Chocolate comes in several different forms. They're not interchangeable. Each recipe is built around a particular kind of chocolate, so it's important to use the exact one that's called for. Most of our recipes use semisweet chocolate, either in chip or 1-ounce-square form. Chocolate chips have many uses besides the traditional chocolate chip cookie. Cocoa also has many uses apart from hot chocolate.

1. Unsweetened chocolate is exactly what it says: there's no sugar added. This type of chocolate is bitter. It comes in individually wrapped 1- or 2-ounce squares or 8- or 9.7-ounce bars. Don't confuse it with semisweet when you bake.

2. Semisweet chocolate, which has sugar added to it, comes in several forms: individually wrapped 1-or 2-ounce squares or 8- or 9.7-ounce bars, various-size baking bars and buttons, chips, and dark chocolate candy bars, such as Hershey's Special Dark, Bourneville Plain and various European chocolate bars, which are available at gourmet shops. Ghirardelli sells semisweet chocolate in 10-pound bars. It's a good way to stuff your face with chocolate without actually knowing how much you've eaten. You'll need a scale to measure it accurately.

3. Bittersweet chocolate has slightly less sugar than semisweet, but the taste is similar. It can be substituted for semisweet chocolate and vice versa, with only a slight change in taste to the end product. It comes in several forms: individually wrapped 1- or 2-ounce squares or 8- or 9.7-ounce bars, various-size baking bars and buttons, and European chocolate bars, which may be labeled "bittersweet" or simply "dark." Bitter-

sweet chocolate, which is high-quality eating chocolate, can be used in all types of desserts.

4. Milk chocolate is very sweet and is not used extensively in baking. It comes in 4-ounce baking bars and chips. We use milk chocolate sparingly in Chocolate Chip Muffins (page 6), Traditional Chocolate Chip Cookies (page 93), and Blondies Topped with Chocolate and Nuts (page 130).

5. White chocolate is technically not chocolate. It is usually made from cocoa butter, milk solids, sugar and flavorings. It comes in various-size baking bars, buttons and chips.

6. Unsweetened cocoa can be used in all types of desserts, not just hot chocolate. It comes in powdered form in boxes and cans and is available in regular and alkalyzed (also called Dutch-process or "European") form. Alkalyzed means that a small amount of alkaline solution has been added to the cocoa to make it smoother, darker and less acidic. Experts say alkalyzed cocoa has a more mellow flavor, but I can't tell the difference.

7. Sweetened cocoa is not used in baked desserts, because it is too sweet and because its chocolate flavor is not as intense as in unsweetened cocoa. It comes in powdered form in cans and packets.

What if I don't have the right kind of chocolate?

Sometimes you can make substitutions, but unless you're an accomplished cook, you're better off making a special trip to get the chocolate that the recipe calls for. The easiest and least risky substitution is using semisweet chocolate chips instead of semisweet or bittersweet squares, although chocolate chips are hard to measure accurately by the teaspoon. But a little extra chocolate won't hurt any recipe. See page 279 for substitutions.

Are "gourmet" cooking chocolates worth it?

Gourmet cooking chocolates, such as Callebaut, Hawaiian Vintage, Scharffen Berger and Valrhona, are high-quality chocolates made for baking and have a higher percentage of cocoa solids than ordinary brands, which means they are richer and more intensely flavored. They can cost up to ten times as much as mass-market brands such as Bakers, Hershey and Nestlé.

In recipes where the flavor of chocolate is prominent, such as Almost Flourless Chocolate Cake (page 35), Flourless Chocolate Mocha Cake (page 44), Chocolate Crème Brûlée (page 168), Foolproof Mini Chocolate Soufflés (page 178), Chocolate-Covered Nuts and Other Goodies (page 242), Truffles (page 252) and hot chocolate (pages 256–58), using the gourmet brands can make a difference.

Experiment to see which brands you prefer. But don't judge them by the way they taste right out of the package; they are often slightly bitter (which sophisticated people seem to like). Use them in recipes, where the richer taste can really make a difference. If gourmet chocolate is not available at local grocery stores or gourmet shops, order it via toll-free numbers or the Internet.

Here are some telephone numbers and Internet addresses:

HAWAIIAN VINTAGE CHOCOLATE
   1-800-345-1543; www.hawaiianchocolate.com

SCHARFFEN BERGER CHOCOLATE
   1-800-930-4528; www.scharffen-berger.com

VALRHONA CHOCOLATE
   www.chocosphere.com

WILLIAMS-SONOMA MAIL ORDER
   1-800-541-2233; www.williams-sonoma.com

What's the best way to melt chocolate?

Next to sitting on it, here's the easiest way to melt chocolate: Put up to 4 ounces in a small, heavy pot; put more than 4 ounces in a heavy frying pan. A cast-iron (or any thick-bottomed) pot or pan will work. Heat the chocolate over very low heat until it is half-melted, stirring constantly with an absolutely dry spoon or spatula. Turn off the heat and let it sit. The residual heat will melt the rest of the chocolate. Do not let any liquid get into the chocolate, unless the recipe tells you otherwise. A drop of water will cause the chocolate to stiffen and become unusable. That's why you should never cover chocolate while it's melting, since steam can condense on the lid and drip into the chocolate.

In general, a microwave oven is best used to heat macaroni and cheese, not chocolate. But here's a good tip from Nestlé: If you want to melt a small amount of chocolate to decorate cookies or a cake, put a handful of chocolate chips in a heavy-duty plastic bag, microwave on high (100%) for 30 to 45 seconds and then squeeze the bag with your fingers. Microwave several more times for 10- to 20-second intervals, kneading in between until the chocolate is melted. Cut a tiny corner from the bag, and squeeze to drizzle over cookies or a cake. For a thicker drizzle, make the hole a little larger.

How do I store chocolate?

Other than in your desk, the easiest and most practical place is at room temperature in a closed cupboard. If you keep it in the refrigerator, moisture may condense on it. Sometimes chocolate will develop a grayish coating, called "bloom," indicating that it has gone through at least one temperature change during storage. Luckily, the taste won't be affected. Just use the chocolate as you normally would. Well-wrapped chocolate should keep for a year, but I've never been able to verify this.

Baking Basics Mom Taught Me

Follow *the* directions.

I know that unquestioningly following directions is the essence of fascism. But baking is apolitical, and changing a recipe's ingredients makes a big difference. It's not like cooking a steak, where you can step on it and throw it down the stairs and it's still going to taste like steak. With baking, things can go wrong if you combine the ingredients in the wrong order. For instance, baking powder and baking soda cause chemical reactions as soon as they get wet, and you want that reaction to happen right before you put the mixture in the oven. So, follow directions as closely as possible. However, when the directions just say to combine a bunch of ingredients in a bowl, you can add them in any order you want.

ALWAYS USE THE RIGHT MEASURING CUPS FOR DRY INGREDIENTS. Being naturally lazy, I used to think that if I got close to the right amount in a recipe, things would work out fine. It turns out that in baking you actually have to pay attention. Those Pyrex measuring cups with the spout? They're only for liquid ingredients. Using them for dry ingredients, particularly flour, can throw things off considerably, because there's no way to measure accurately. How can you level off the top with a knife—the key to all successful baking—when the Pyrex cup is only half full? This is the number-one reason that people mess up.

ALWAYS PREHEAT THE OVEN. Some ovens heat faster than others. To standardize the timing, it's best if the oven has reached the right temperature by the time you start baking.

DON'T BLINDLY TRUST YOUR OVEN. The temperature dial may be lying, reading 350° when it's actually 400°. You can outsmart it by buying a $10 oven thermometer.

BAKE IN THE MIDDLE OF THE OVEN. Air can circulate better in the middle and there are less likely to be hot spots, so baked goods are less likely to burn. Ovens generally have two racks that can be adjusted to different positions. Some just slide right out, while others require a series of contortions to remove. Occasionally, you might have to use both racks at once, but ideally you will use only one. If possible, bake cookies one sheet at a time—don't stack them. Cookies need personal space.

DON'T OPEN THE OVEN EVERY FIVE MINUTES to see if what you're baking is done—you may ruin it, since cooler air from outside the oven can lower the temperature inside and throw the timing off. Opening the oven once should be enough, about five or ten minutes before your baking is supposed to be done.

Know your ingredients.

BUTTER/MARGARINE/SHORTENING

For ease of preparation, **butter** and **margarine** should always be used at room temperature, unless they are going to be melted, and then it doesn't matter. One way to soften butter or margarine quickly is to peel it into thin sheets using a vegetable peeler. The easiest way, though, is to take it out of the refrigerator an hour before you need it — if you can plan that far ahead.

Since you asked, my mom and I always use butter instead of margarine because of the taste. I've never eaten either one raw, but there's no comparison between the taste of baked goods with butter and those with margarine. And in terms of healthfulness, the experts have gone back and forth. The bottom line is they're both fat, so build your diet around a moderate consumption of either one.

If possible, use **unsalted butter**, because it has the sweetest, purest, fullest flavor. That's because the salt added to butter is used as a preservative, and therefore unsalted butter is probably fresher. To confuse you, salted butter is often labeled "sweet butter," but unsalted butter is always labeled "unsalted." All this being said, I've used both salted and unsalted butter in baking without any discernible difference in taste. One caution: don't use whipped butter or soft tub margarine, because they have air and/or water beaten into them and will not produce the same results.

Shortening, such as Crisco, comes in a can and can be stored in a cupboard rather than the refrigerator. I tried it in one recipe but didn't like the result. I guess it's a matter of personal preference.

SUGAR

White sugar, which is also called granulated sugar, or just plain sugar, is the most common sugar used in baking. It also comes in cubes, but that's mostly to feed horses. Stick to the bags of loose sugar.

Powdered (confectioners') sugar is white sugar that has been ground so fine that it looks like powder. A small amount of cornstarch has been added to keep the grains from sticking together. It is not a good substitute for granulated sugar, except when sweetening whipped cream.

Brown sugar comes in light and dark versions. Because dark brown sugar has a stronger taste due to its higher molasses content, I usually opt for light brown. However, the two can be used interchangeably.

Occasionally, if you don't close the package tightly, brown sugar becomes a block of granite. My instinct is to hack at the lump with a knife until it's in small-enough pieces to use. But my mom advises putting it on a cookie sheet and heating it in the oven at 250° for about 5 minutes. Or use a bizarre home remedy that defies science: Transfer the sugar to a glass jar with a tight lid and add a quarter of an apple, which will soften it within a few days.

Eggs

When I first started baking, I didn't realize that eggs were sorted by sizes: jumbo (which are as big as ostrich eggs), extra-large, large, medium and small. Large eggs tend to be the most common and most prominently placed in stores. We call for these in our recipes. The color of the shell doesn't matter — brown eggs and white eggs are the same inside.

Some of our recipes call for egg yolks or egg whites only. That means you will have to separate the eggs. Here's how you do it (keep in mind that it's easier to separate eggs when they are cold): Have two bowls ready. Crack the egg firmly against the edge of one bowl; the eggshell should break in half across the middle. Separate the two halves, turning them both upright over the bowl you want to contain the white. Let the white dribble into the bowl, keeping the yolk in one upright shell. By carefully transferring the yolk back and forth between the shell halves, you can allow gravity to draw the white into the bowl. Your goal here is to avoid breaking the yolk. If any drops of yolk get into the white, spoon them out, or the beaten whites won't fluff up properly.

Flour

All of our recipes call for **all-purpose flour**. **Cake flour,** which is widely available in the South, is lighter than all-purpose flour and is said to make cakes more tender. If you want to use cake flour in our cake recipes, add 2 tablespoons more flour for each cup of flour called for. **Bread flour** is specifically for bread and should not be used for recipes in this book. Bleached or unbleached? It really doesn't matter.

To measure flour, spoon it into a measuring cup — do not scoop it out of the container with the measuring cup itself — and level the top with a knife. Don't pack the flour into the cup, or your baked product will be so heavy it will bend the oven rack.

Salt

A small amount of salt brings out the flavor of other ingredients; a lot ruins the recipe. Don't get carried away.

Baking Powder/Baking Soda

Baking powder and baking soda are leavening agents, which means they magically cause baked products to rise. They are usually added near the end of a recipe, because as soon as they come into contact with liquid, they begin to do their job. Once a package of either of these is opened, it usually lasts for about six months. Check the use-by date on the package. Or if there's no date, dissolve ¼ teaspoon of the powder or soda in a cup of water. If it fizzes, it's fine. If it doesn't, get a fresh container.

CREAM OF TARTAR

Cream of tartar, a white powder, is mainly used to help egg whites maintain their fluffiness when beaten; it is unrelated to tartar sauce, the seafood condiment. Add a small amount of cream of tartar to the egg whites when they become bubbly, but before they have been beaten into stiff peaks. It is available in bottles in the spice rack at the grocery store or supermarket.

CREAM/MILK

All our recipes call for **heavy cream**, which is usually available in the dairy case in half-pint (8-ounce) and pint (16-ounce) containers. Heavy cream may also be called "**heavy whipping cream**." Other creams include **light cream** and **half-and-half**; they cannot be substituted for heavy cream.

Whipped cream doesn't just come out of aerosol cans. Here's how to make a much better tasting version, and it only takes 5 minutes.

To make whipped cream: About 10 minutes before you plan to whip the cream, put the beaters of your electric mixer and a bowl in the freezer (the cream will whip faster if your utensils are cold). Pour the cream into the bowl, and beat with an electric mixer until it thickens and forms stiff peaks, 1 to 2 minutes (longer if the cream, beaters and bowl are not ice-cold). Whipping cream in a food processor won't work, but you can use an eggbeater or a whisk; the latter will take more time.

Milk is available in four choices: whole milk, 2% fat, 1% fat and nonfat (skim). I use skim. Choose whatever makes you moo.

Buttermilk used to be what was left over in the churn after butter was made, but now it's made commercially by adding a bacterial culture to nonfat milk. It sounds gross, but buttermilk makes especially tender baked goods and is an essential ingredient in several of our recipes, including Four-Layer Buttermilk Chocolate Cake (page 49). Buttermilk is available in cartons near regular milk.

Evaporated milk comes in 5- and 14½-ounce cans. It's milk with 60 percent of the water removed, which makes it thicker and richer than fresh milk. It can be diluted and substituted for fresh milk, although the flavor may be slightly different. It lasts a lot longer than regular milk, which makes it very convenient. We use it in our recipe for Orange Fudge (page 246) instead of cream. It is usually available in your supermarket's baking section (or in a special section of canned and powdered milk).

Sweetened condensed milk comes in 15-ounce cans. It's similar to evaporated milk but has a lot of sugar added. It is often used in making fudge, cream pies and puddings. It is usually available in your supermarket's baking section (or in a special section of canned and powdered milk). Don't substitute evaporated milk.

Vanilla and Other Extracts

Vanilla extract is an alcoholic substance with a vanilla flavor. The vanilla adds a subtle flavor, and the alcohol brings out the flavor of chocolate. I prefer "pure vanilla extract" to "imitation vanilla," just on principle. If you happen to run out of vanilla, you can substitute an equivalent amount of rum, whiskey, cognac or any flavored liqueur that you happen to be hiding in your apron.

Almond, peppermint and **cherry extracts** are available in your supermarket's baking section, near the vanilla. These extracts should be used sparingly, or you'll never get the taste out of your mouth.

Nuts

You can toast nuts in a single layer on a cookie sheet in a 350° oven for about 5 minutes to bring out their flavor. Nuts can be chopped in a food processor or by hand with a sharp knife. Or you can put them in a heavy-duty, self-sealing plastic bag and hit them with a rolling pin or heavy can until they are the size you want. If you grind nuts in a food processor, don't process them too long, or they will turn into nut butter. Processing them along with any sugar called for in the recipe helps prevent this.

I've never had nuts go bad on me, but my mom is extra cautious and freezes them. In my opinion, life is too short to bother with storing nuts in the freezer.

Key Weights & Measures

Dash = 1/16 teaspoon

3 teaspoons = 1 tablespoon

4 tablespoons = ¼ cup

8 tablespoons = ½ cup

1 stick butter = ½ cup = 8 tablespoons

1 cup = 8 fluid ounces = ½ pint

16 ounces = 1 pound

1 quart = 2 pints = 4 cups

1 pound flour = 3½ cups

1 pound granulated sugar = 2 cups

1 pound brown sugar = 2¼ cups

1 pound powdered (confectioners') sugar = 4 cups

1 tablespoon cornstarch = 2 tablespoons flour

1 cup walnut pieces = 4 ounces shelled walnuts

Chocolate Equivalents

1 cup chocolate chips = 6-ounce package chocolate chips

1 cup semisweet chocolate chips = 6 ounces semisweet chocolate

1 (1-ounce) square = 4 teaspoons (1 ounce) chips

1½ (1-ounce) squares = ¼ cup (1½ ounces) chips

3 (1-ounce) squares = ½ cup (3 ounces) chips

6 (1-ounce) squares = 1 cup (6 ounces) chips

1 (1-ounce) square unsweetened chocolate = 3 tablespoons unsweetened cocoa + 1 tablespoon butter

1 (1-ounce) square unsweetened chocolate = 2 (1-ounce) squares semisweet chocolate without the 2 tablespoons sugar called for in the recipe

1 (1-ounce) square semisweet chocolate = ½ (1-ounce) square unsweetened chocolate + 1 tablespoon sugar

Index

Almond Crunch, Chocolate, 248

Almost Flourless Chocolate Cake, 36

Apricots, Chocolate-Dipped/Frozen
   Chocolate Banana Slices, 189

Bagels, Chocolate Chip Mini-, 10

Banana
   Bread, Chocolate, 4
   Cake, Fabulous Four Seasons, 211
   Slices, Frozen Chocolate/Chocolate-
      Dipped Apricots, 189

Bars, Congo, 126

Basic Chocolate Fondue, 193

Biscotti, Chocolate-Dipped, 112

Bittersweet Dessert Sauce, 231

Bread, Chocolate Banana, 4

Bread Pudding, Chocolate, 181

Breakfast Cake, Orange-Chocolate, 18

Breakfast dishes
   Baby Brioches, Chocolate-Filled, 14
   Banana Bread, Chocolate, 4
   Cake, Orange-Chocolate Breakfast, 18
   Mini-Bagels, Chocolate Chip, 10

Muffins, Chocolate Chip, 6

Rugelach, Chocolate Chip, 25

Scones, Chocolate Chip, 8

Waffles, Chocolate, 22

Brioches, Chocolate-Filled Baby, 14

Brownie(s)
   Chocolate Oatmeal, 132
   Cookies, 75
   Fudge Pie, 137
   Gooey Double-Chocolate Pudding, 184
   Intensely Chocolate Cocoa, 128
   Macaroons, 120
   Movie Star, 122
   Peanut Butter Chocolate, 134
   Triple Chocolate, 119

Butter Cookies, Chocolate, 78

Buttermilk Chocolate Cake, Four-Layer, 53

Cake
   Almost Flourless Chocolate, 35
   Chocolate Mousse, 38
   Chocolate Polenta, 41
   Chocolate Pound, 46

Devil's Food, 55
Fabulous Four Seasons Banana, 211
Flourless Chocolate Mocha, 44
Four-Layer Buttermilk Chocolate, 49
Marble Cheesecake, 62
Orange-Chocolate Breakfast, 18
Raspberry Chocolate Pudding, 208
Sachertorte, 64
You-Deserve-It Fudge, 57
Can't-Fail Pie Crust, 151
Candied Orange Peel, 21
Candy
    Chocolate Almond Crunch, 248
    Nuts and Other Goodies, Chocolate-
        Covered, 241
    Orange Fudge, 245
    Peanut Butter and Chocolate Chunks,
        250
    Surprisingly Easy Fudge, 243
    Truffles, 252
Cheesecake, Marble, 69
Cherry-Chocolate Truffle Pie, 219
Chocolate Chip
    Cookies
        Double-Sided Double, 105
        Peanut Butter, 99
        Traditional, 93

Crisp, Peachy, 202
Cupcakes, Grandma's, 32
Meringues, Positively Sinful, 96
Mini-Bagels, 10
Muffins, 6
Rugelach, 25
Scones, 8
Cocoa
    Brownies, Intensely Chocolate, 114
    Crust, Easy, 163
Coconut Macaroons, Chocolate, 80
Congo Bars, 112
Cookie(s)
    Biscotti, Chocolate-Dipped, 112
    Brownie, 75
    Chocolate Butter, 78
    Chocolate Chip Peanut Butter, 107
    Chocolate Coconut Macaroons, 81
    Chocolate Shortbread, 93
    Chocolate Thumbprints, 85
    Double-Sided Double Chocolate Chip,
        116
    Dough Pie Crust, 159
    Florentines, 95
    Lava, 88
    Spicy Chocolate, 91
    Traditional Chocolate Chip, 99

Couldn't-Be-Simpler Chocolate Icing, 72
Creamy Chocolate Mousse, 170
Crème Brûlée, Chocolate, 167
Crêpes, Chocolate Dessert, 195
Crisp, Peachy Chocolate Chip, 203
Crumb Crust, Chocolate, 154
Crunch, Chocolate Almond, 248
Crust, Pie
    Can't-Fail, 151
    Chocolate Crumb, 154
    Cookie Dough, 159
    Easy Cocoa, 162
    Peanutty, 156
Cupcakes
    Grandma's Chocolate Chip, 32
    Overly Indulgent Chocolate, 30

Dessert Sauce. See also Sauce, Chocolate
    Bittersweet, 231
Devil's Food Cake, 61
Double-Sided Double Chocolate Chip
    Cookies, 116

Fabulous Four Seasons Banana Cake, 211
Florentines, 95
Flourless Chocolate Mocha Cake, 47
Fondue, Chocolate, 191

Basic, 193
Mint, 193
Mocha, 193
Peanut Butter and, 194
Foolproof Mini Chocolate Soufflés with
    Chocolate Sauce, 178
Four-Layer Buttermilk Chocolate Cake, 53
Fresh Strawberry Meringues Drizzled with
    Chocolate, 205
Frozen Chocolate Banana
    Slices/Chocolate-Dipped Apricots, 189
Fudge
    Cake, You-Deserve-It, 57
    Orange, 245
    Pie, Brownie, 137
    Sauce, Hot, 237
    Surprisingly Easy, 243

Ganache, 70
Gooey Double-Chocolate Brownie
    Pudding, 184
Grandma's Chocolate Chip Cupcakes, 32

Hot Chocolate
    Mexican, 257
    Parisian, 255
Hot Fudge Sauce, 237

Ice Cream Sandwiches, Minty, 227
Icing
    Chocolate Buttercream, 68
    Couldn't-Be-Simpler Chocolate, 72
    Easy Chocolate Glaze, 66
    Ganache, 70
    Quick Fudge, 72
Incredibly Easy Chocolate Mousse, 172
Instant Chocolate Mousse Fix, 174
Intensely Chocolate Cocoa Brownies, 128

Lava Cookies, 88
Low-Fat Creamy Chocolate Yogurt, 176

Macaroons
    Brownie, 120
    Chocolate Coconut, 81
Marble Cheesecake, 69
Meringue(s)
    Fresh Strawberry, Drizzled with
        Chocolate, 205
    Pie, Chocolate, 143
    Positively Sinful Chocolate Chip, 104
Mexican Hot Chocolate, 257
Miniature Chocolate Turnovers, 149
Mini-Bagels, Chocolate Chip, 10
Mint Fondue, Chocolate, 193

Minty Ice Cream Sandwiches, 227
Mocha
    Cake, Flourless Chocolate, 47
    Fondue, Chocolate, 193
    Sauce, Chocolate-, 233
Mousse, Chocolate
    Cake, 39
    Creamy, 170
    Incredibly Easy, 172
    Instant Fix, 174
    Pie, 139
Movie Star Brownies, 122
Muffins, Chocolate Chip, 6

Nuts and Other Goodies, Chocolate-
    Covered, 241

Oatmeal Brownies, Chocolate, 132
Orange
    -Chocolate Breakfast Cake, 18
    Peel, Candied, 21
Overly Indulgent Chocolate Cupcakes, 29

Parisian Hot Chocolate, 255
Peachy Chocolate Chip Crisp, 203
Peanut Butter
    and Chocolate Chunks, 250

Peanut Butter (*cont.*)
   and Chocolate Fondue, 194
   Chocolate Brownies, 134
   Cookies, Chocolate Chip, 107
Peanutty Pie Crust, 156
Pecan Pie, Chocolate, 141
Pie(s)
   Brownie Fudge, 138
   Cherry-Chocolate Truffle, 215
   Chocolate Angel, 144
   Chocolate Meringue, 144
   Chocolate Mousse, 140
   Chocolate Pecan, 142
   Chocolate Strawberry, 217
Pie Crust(s)
   Can't-Fail, 152
   Chocolate Crumb, 155
   Cookie Dough, 160
   Easy Cocoa, 163
   Peanutty, 157
Pizza, Chocolate, 219
Polenta Cake, Chocolate, 43
Positively Sinful Chocolate Chip
   Meringues, 96
Pound Cake, Chocolate, 46
Pudding
   Bread, Chocolate, 181

Brownie, Gooey Double-Chocolate, 184
Cake, Raspberry Chocolate, 208

Raspberry
   Chocolate Pudding Cake, 208
   Chocolate Tart, 214
   Sauce, 25
Rugelach, Chocolate Chip, 26

Sachertorte, 64
Sauce
   Bittersweet Dessert, 231
   Chocolate-Mocha, 233
   Foolproof Mini Chocolate Soufflés with
      Chocolate, 178
   Hot Fudge, 237
   Raspberry, 25
Scones, Chocolate Chip, 8
Shortbread Cookies, Chocolate, 93
Shortcake, Chocolate Strawberry, 200
Soda, Untraditional Chocolate, 260
Soufflés with Chocolate Sauce, Foolproof
   Mini Chocolate, 178
Spicy Chocolate Cookies, 91
Strawberry
   Meringues Drizzled with Chocolate,
      Fresh, 204

Pie, Chocolate, 221
  Shortcake, Chocolate, 200
Surprisingly Easy Fudge, 243
Syrup, Chocolate, 235

Tart, Raspberry Chocolate, 214
Thumbprints, Chocolate, 85
Traditional Chocolate Chip Cookies, 99
Triple Chocolate Brownies, 119
Truffle Pie, Cherry-Chocolate, 219

Truffles, 252
Turnovers, Miniature Chocolate, 149

Untraditional Chocolate Soda, 260

Waffles, Chocolate, 22

Yogurt, Low-Fat Creamy Chocolate, 176
You-Deserve-It Fudge Cake, 57

About the Authors

Kevin Mills, a history graduate of Cornell University, lives in Los Angeles, where he is a writer.

Nancy Mills, a home economics graduate of Cornell University, writes for such publications as the *Los Angeles Times, New York Daily News, San Francisco Chronicle* and *USA Weekend*. She also co-owns a newspaper feature syndicate.

Kevin and Nancy's two previous collaborations are *HELP! My Apartment Has a Kitchen* and *HELP! My Apartment Has a Dining Room*. They also co-author "You Gotta Eat," a weekly column for Tribune Media.